Found

Found Out

Transgressive Faith and Sexuality

Alison Webster

DARTON·LONGMAN+TODD

First published in Great Britain in 2017 by
Darton, Longman and Todd Ltd
1 Spencer Court
140–142 Wandsworth High Street
London SW18 4JJ

© 2017 Alison Webster

The right of Alison Webster to be identified as the Author of this work has been asserted in accordance with the Copyright, Designs and Patents Act 1988

ISBN 978-0-232-53263-0

A catalogue record for this book is available from the British Library

Phototypeset by Kerrypress Ltd, St Albans
Printed and bound by Bell & Bain, Glasgow

Contents

Acknowledgements		vii
Testimonials		ix
Introduction		1
Chapter One	Found Out	7
Chapter Two	Retrospective	17
Chapter Three	Resistance	43
Chapter Four	Reclaiming Spirit	79
Chapter Five	Recreating Faith	103
Chapter Six	Remaking Love	125
Conclusion		147
Notes		155

Acknowledgements

This book would not have come into being without the women at the heart of LEFT (Lesbians Exploring Faith Together). It was their idea to host a conference in November 2015 to mark the twentieth anniversary of the publication of my book, *Found Wanting: Women, Christianity and Sexuality*. Feeling that much has changed for women and for LGBT people over those twenty years, it seemed timely to explore that terrain. With a panel made up of Rachel Mann, Rosie Miles and Savitri Hensman, and a full-house of some 45 women, we began the task of reflecting together on the themes of spirituality, sexuality and social change. By the end of the day I was buzzing with the amazing stories told and reflections offered. A couple of days later, on the train to work, I was struck by the idea of delving into these things more deeply, with the help perhaps of some of those who had been present, reaching out also to others who were not. Thus I was given the idea of *Found Out: Transgressive Faith and Sexuality*.

Thanks first and foremost to the women who have contributed directly to this book – in writing and through conversation. We are young and old, Black and White, lesbian and straight (and various shades in between), trans and cis. We have a range of health and disability issues affecting our embodiment, and some are survivors of various forms of abuse, including sexual abuse. We are clergy and lay, and we come from a diverse range of faith perspectives. It has been a privilege and a challenge to hear the stories, to find out much that is new to me, and to weave it all together to produce *Found Out*.

I have very much appreciated and depended upon the support of my two families: the Websters and the Okafors. The former for space in Norfolk to hide away; the latter for cutting me the slack to do that. Special thanks to Ben Okafor for being able to hear what I'm not saying; for understanding the turns of my heart and my spirit, and for inspiring me with your own artistry, and your idiosyncratic approach to scripture and faith.

LEFT has had an ongoing and very supportive role, allowing me to test out ideas at the annual retreat, then subsequently to share some of my reflections from the finished work. You are an amazing group of women.

In the closing stages, two people emerged as astute and wise readers of my drafts, offering me prompt and crucial feedback and ideas that – as they will see – have made a considerable difference to what is said and how. So, my heartfelt appreciation goes out to Anne Richards and Bob Armstrong.

Finally, thanks to DLT for taking on this project with such an enthusiastic welcome.

Testimonials

'Reading this book is a profound, I would say, sacramental experience. By hearing into speech the compelling stories of a range of extraordinary women, Webster reveals the Christ who transgresses all boundaries and invites us to play with him on the edges of our identities. Webster offers some signposts for the Church as it attempts to reverse itself out of the cul-de-sac it is currently caught up in over issues of sexuality. Such a journey will involve turning from systems into the faces of those marginalised by them, but in those faces we will find the Christ who waits for us all with love, forgiveness and hope.'
     Professor Elizabeth Stuart, Deputy Vice-Chancellor,
              University of Winchester

'This book is the outcome of a remarkable project in practical theology. Alison Webster, displaying an exceptional ability to put her contributors at ease, has listened with disciplined attentiveness to the voices of a group of passionate women who dare to give authentic expression to their deepest thoughts and feelings about their spiritual and sexual experience. They show how much institutional religion can stifle and even demonise the most inspirational insights and cast agonising doubt on the validity of subjective experience.

 If the churches facilitated conversations of this kind instead of running scared of difference and emotional honesty, we should be well on the way to embracing a way of being based on the unconditional love of God and our own infinite belovedness.'
  Professor Brian Thorne, Co-founder, The Norwich Centre for
  Personal, Professional and Spiritual Development and Lay
              Canon, Norwich Cathedral

'For much of its history the development of Christianity has operated on the basis that the abstract mattered more than the concrete, theories were more important than people, order more so than liberation. This book represents everything that is good about the emerging transgressive queering of faith and praxis that is challenging the church and transforming ordinary lives from the bottom up. Alison Webster's book is an incisive, readable commentary on the changes in the wider culture and within the church over the past 30 years. It is the perfect antidote for the ungenerous, grim realities of post-Brexit Britain with which we must all do battle.'

Anthony G. Reddie, Extraordinary Professor with the University of South Africa and a Learning and Development Officer for the Methodist Church. He is also the editor of *Black Theology: An International Journal*

'*Found Out* is a beautiful book. It has all of Alison Webster's hallmarks: the interweaving of poetry; biblical meditation; theological, sociological and psychological theory; her own story and the stories of others. I marvelled at Webster's work of listening and community-building: how present and how trusted she must have been to draw these stories out. *Found Out* is a painful read but it is ultimately hopeful. It demonstrates how theological thinking on sexuality can be done and offers us all a way forward. It is brilliant work. Alison Webster is a true thinker-feeler-humaniser-prophet.'

Jo Ind, writer

'*Found Out* is an invaluable book for anyone seeking an authentic relationship with God. With courage and piercing insight, Webster engages multiple perspectives – in real women's own voices – to see how the sacred is lived, loved, and accessed in today's world, sometimes inside church walls and often not. In this powerful testimony, the persistent quest to find connection with the sacred leaps off the page. *Found Out* offers rich fields to explore for those of us in the business of opening pathways to God.'

The Rev. Elizabeth M. Edman, author of *Queer Virtue: What LGBTQ People Know About Life and Love and How It Can Revitalize Christianity*

'Alison Webster faithfully conveys the stories of myriad women and their friends who push well beyond heteronormative and religious boundaries to explore how spirituality, sexuality, and social change configure contemporary relational landscapes. She writes compellingly about the centrality of tears, queer theory, situated theologies, and the need to prize not judge differences. Trust women to be themselves, she urges, and imagine how good the world could be without abuse and oppression. This is a volume to ponder and share, internalize and discuss.'

Mary Hunt, theologian and co-director of WATER (Women's Alliance for Theology, Ethics, and Ritual), USA

'Theology for Alison Webster is not a sport or hobby. It is survival. Driven by the hard realities of experience and the imperative of injustice, she fearlessly dusts off the sources, norms and ends of theological imagining to reconstruct liberation and hope for those whose voice is seldom heard. If the Church, poised on its various tightropes, is trying to balance so hard that it becomes incapable of moving, then this is a timely book that interrupts our paralysis in the name of God, calling us out, like Lazarus, to find ourselves loved to the point of tears.'

Mark Oakley, Chancellor of St Paul's Cathedral

'With great sensitivity Alison Webster captures the confessions of those caught between norms of church or society and the realities of their lives, identities and sexualities. Out of this tension come bold and hard-won insights about church, spirituality and scripture.

Caught at a moment of history which has cost them a great deal, their faith shines through.'
Linda Woodhead, Professor, Department of Politics, Philosophy and Religion, Lancaster University

Introduction

Reflection

Jesus asked you a question at dinner, 'Simon, do you see this woman?' It was really four questions.

'Simon, do YOU see this woman?' You. Do you see her? Simon, the Pharisee. Religious leader. One with authority. Why did you invite Jesus to eat with you? Simply because you could, probably. And why did he accept? Because he thought you had things to learn. But you didn't seem like someone who wanted to learn, you seemed like someone who wanted only to teach, to tell, to impose. You betrayed yourself when you told Jesus, 'Speak', when he had something to say to you. He didn't need your permission and didn't seek it, but you gave it to him anyway.

'Simon, do you SEE this woman?' Did you even see her, or was she just the pretext for an argument – a convenient thing to be used? You were looking AT her, not really seeing. You made a lot of assumptions, but you didn't ask her anything. Didn't you wonder why she was there? Why she was crying? I suppose the fact that you had labelled her 'a sinner' meant that no further questions were needed.

'Simon, do you see THIS woman?' That one. There. In your house. In that moment. Not the whole category of women in general; not a nameless specimen of the generic, but that particular person. Someone with an identity and a story; someone who had loved and been loved. Someone whom God still loved.

'Simon, do you see this WOMAN?' This woman. Did you appreciate what it meant to be female in your context? To be subject to the rule of men, with little freedom or self-determination?

Introduction

What must it have cost her to come to your house that day? She knew her reputation; she knew that you knew. She must have imagined the looks she would get from you and your friends – the disdain, the opprobrium. She saw something in Jesus that made her think he would be different, but she couldn't know for sure. What if he rejected her too? What if he thought she was simply making an embarrassing spectacle of herself?

Nevertheless, she took the risk and came with a symbolic gift to lay before one she instinctively trusted with herself – perfume and tears.

And he saw her. Jesus SAW her. He saw HER.

This is a book about experience, and reality. It is not theoretical or academic, though it does involve complex ideas. It is based on my experience and my context and it is written from my heart and my spirit. There is much of me in it, but it is not about me. Ultimately, this book is built on conversations that go back decades. More immediately and recently, though, I have spoken face to face – and sometimes by email and online – with women from a range of backgrounds and faith perspectives. Their experiences have been freely and generously shared. I use only first names, and all names have been changed. I hope I have listened carefully, and communicated with integrity. The task has been a privilege and an honour. I see this book as an exercise in practical theology. It is not 'about' theologies of sexuality and gender so much as a bringing together of experience with aspects of scripture and the Christian tradition that might, at best, help to inform it. Often the theological resources that should feed us have been deployed against us, alienating us from the potential riches of our various traditions. We have had to find ways to reinhabit them.

It is a book that combines narrative with reflections, stories, and occasionally poetry (usually when the contributors have found poetry the best way to express themselves). The reflections often take the form of engagements with scripture or an aspect of the Christian tradition. They are intended to be suggestive and exploratory, raising themes and ideas in an oblique way – themes that will be returned to in the subsequent narrative. The intention is to open up the various meanings and connections that you, the reader, might make between the reflection and your own experience. As the author I cannot know your experience, and do not want try to direct or dictate the connections that you will make.

Likewise with the stories I tell which, for me, enable us to look at ideas from new angles. They can enhance the ideas being explored, and ground them in experience. But again, you will not find me explaining what the stories *mean* or why I have chosen to tell them. That is your work.

The contributors' stories fall mainly into two sections, Chapter Three (Resistance) and Chapter Four (Reclaiming Spirit), though they are woven into other parts of the book too. I have chosen to leave them as free-flowing as possible, with any commentary serving only to ease the flow. There is a certain momentum and pace achieved by the voices coming one after another. Each person has a unique style, and hearing these differences is like being in a room and being part of a discussion. Again, you will sense resonances and make connections between your life and theirs, and I do not want to get in the way of that process. My job is to pull out what I consider to be key and crucial themes in the overall exploration of what we, as women, have found out about ourselves – our identities, our faith, our ways of embracing God, our ways of allowing ourselves to be accepted and loved by God.

There is so much depth and richness in the stories offered by the contributors to this book. And the theological nuances and spiritual subtleties that flow from them engender in me a passionate frustration that mainstream denominations, on the whole, have no place for them.

This is not a book about the churches – their various policies and practices relating to gender and sexuality. But it would be impossible, and wrong, to ignore the institutional church backdrop against which many women have plotted their journeys – the seemingly implacable Christian institutions that have for many remained hostile, inhospitable, insecure and unsafe places. Pamela Lightsey offers the following diagnosis:

'The current crisis of the Church surrounding sexuality will continue because our conversations are often not guided by faith but by the will to control. This will, at its core, springs forth from fear of the unknown. Unfortunately, when discussing sexuality too many Christians of all stripes fail to put to full use all theological sources and fail to enter the discussion humbly. Mostly, what they do is apply scripture not in order to *find out* but in order to *tell why*. This is oppression clothed in religiosity. Guided by fear of sexuality, the ultimate human existential unknown condition, we dig deep into our positions and refuse simply to say, "I don't know". Admitting what we don't know will free us to work with what we do know. Because we don't fully understand human sexuality, what can we do with what we know? Begin by loving ourselves as God created us.'[1]

I have had church variously described to me as 'psychologically pernicious' (in relation to the 'don't ask don't tell' nature of the church's policy towards gay and lesbian clergy) and 'devious' (in relation to the low-grade sexism and sexual harassment which women in ministry experience, and the fact that it can't be reported because the people who perpetrate it are 'not bad people'). So much is unspoken and half-spoken, and truth is elusive.

Inevitably most of these critiques are directed at the most powerful denomination in our context – the Church of England. Having observed this denomination at close quarters, and worked within it for almost two decades, I count myself as an outsider with an insider's perspective. My sense is that around thirty years ago the Church of England allowed itself to be manoeuvred into a theo-political cul-de-sac. There was a combination of reasons for this, too complex to go into here, but the avoidance of schism over approaches to LGBT issues was perhaps the most prominent.

Introduction

Our social context has changed immeasurably, as described in Chapter Two (Retrospective). Most people now think there is a need to get out of the cul-de-sac. Indeed, there's a recognition that this should have happened years ago. The world looks on and wonders why Christians are apparently so frightened of diversity – unable to embrace a world of non-binaries, fluidity and the celebration of love wherever it is found. What's more, they are bewildered that, in a world that needs more love, not less, in the name of a God Christians declare to *be* love, some manifestations of it are proscribed, crushed and disqualified. And all because we are apparently imprisoned by our power structures and bamboozled by our own internal politics.

My hope lies in the fact that this situation cannot and will not last. One day, the Church of England will have to come out and make its home in the mainstream. It will need to admit that it stopped engaging with other disciplines on gender and sexuality, and neglected to listen to the wider world and notice God at work there. It did this because it thought it had a privileged access to the truth. And it will need to acknowledge that what it thought God had intended to be unchanging and static is actually – just like everything else in God's creation – made for diversity, unpredictability and freedom. If it chooses, the church could emerge, chastened but unbowed, declaring a desire to learn, to listen and to change. This is what I believe the vast majority within it would like to see happen.

Structural evil is ever-present in human institutions, and always will be. Jesus lived with evil structures. So do we. Evil structures are usually held in place and maintained by good people. Lovely people, even. That's the irony. Lovely people can become the baying crowd calling for crucifixion, or the leaders that fail to step in to prevent it, for fear of their own lives and positions. Many leaders could have done better in preventing us from entering the cul-de-sac, and in helping us out of it earlier. But we are where we are. The job is still there to be done, and I have deep compassion for those to whom it falls. I work day to day with those who bear the responsibility and feel the pain of having to implement structural injustice: Diocesan Directors of Ordinands, for instance, who are required to ask candidates to sign up to the church's so-called teaching on sexuality as outlined in *Issues in Human Sexuality* (IHS)[2] (the discussion paper that has congealed into doctrine because nobody took an explicit decision that it should not). And those who select and train people for Licensed Lay Ministry who are aware of implementing the opposite: a ruling that contradicts IHS, which said that there was no bar on lay people being in gay and lesbian relationships. But their approximation to ordained ministers has trumped their identity as lay. And bishops and senior clergy who, by the force of an imposed collegiality, may not be honest in public about their feelings and thoughts.

My aim is to show how structures of thought and imagination provide invisible cages that we bump into constantly and painfully – and differently, depending on where we are positioned in those structures. To dismantle them, we need to understand them. To understand them we need to talk to one another, openly and honestly, about how it feels for us. Those who hold power within the institution may find it harder to see the cage, but they are nevertheless imprisoned by it, and any liberation will be for them too. Liberation, perhaps, from being seduced into being the source of stability and order in a world that seemingly has no centre, when what people want from them is a sense that they find and maintain their centre in God who holds all things together. Simply that. My conviction is that all those who bear the pain of this structural dysfunction will eventually unite to dismantle it. The 'us' and 'them' is breaking down, and change is going to come. Very soon.

Chapter One

Found Out

'Tis mercy all, immense and free;
For, O my God, it found out me.'
(Charles Wesley)

Reflection

Why did you weep?

Down the centuries, religious people have seen no mystery here. Your friend Lazarus had died. His family (also your close friends) were distraught. And you were late turning up. The implication is that his death was somehow your fault. You could have prevented it. So what have they said, these wise commentators? That you wept for loss, for compassion, but also for regret – a sense of guilt at your own negligence. You wept with empathy on seeing the impact of the loss on Mary and Martha, both of whom you loved deeply, though in very different ways.

But that doesn't really work, does it? You healed others from a distance – the Centurion's servant, for instance, why not Lazarus? You could have said the word, and the healing would have happened. We know that was within your power. And you could have changed your plans and returned to Bethany, had you chosen to. But you didn't. You chose to wait. And when you arrived, you knew his death was temporary. You felt their sadness, but you knew it would soon be turned into joy.

So I ask again. Why did you weep?

I think you wept because in that moment, you were powerfully reconnected with your sense of calling and purpose. It was a bit like the moment of your baptism when the dove descended and God spoke to reassure: 'This is my beloved. Listen to him.' The tears were transcendent – a sign that you flowed in God and God flowed in you and the result was that you brought both freedom and mercy. Freedom from death, and mercy in life. Your task was to manifest this in your lifetime, and witness to the rest of us that this is possible also for us, if we embrace the Spirit: to be merciful, compassionate, life-giving.

You wept.

Story

Walking through the city of Norwich, I encountered a preacher in the public square. Supported by others who were giving out leaflets from their makeshift stall, he was shouting to passers-by about the love of God. His tone was hectoring. He could not emphasise loudly (and to my ears, harshly) enough how much God loves people, and has given his life for them 'in Jesus Christ'. I grimaced as I always do in these situations, embarrassed by the tone, the content, the very fact that this would be perceived by many as Christianity in action. As I hurried on by, hasty to be out of earshot, a young busker a few hundred yards further on struck up a song on his acoustic guitar. It was the famous 'Hallelujah' by Leonard Cohen. He sang, gently, about doing his best, about it not being much, of not being able to feel, but trying to touch; and declaring that even though it had all gone wrong, he could stand before the Lord of song, with nothing on his tongue but 'Hallelujah'.

It seemed like a parable, and it brought tears to my eyes. The juxtaposition told the story of two very different ways of being in the world. One quiet, creative and humble, the other assertive and bullying, an invasion of others' space. I felt encroached upon by the preacher – disregarded, depersonalised and objectified. Yet the musician's gentle invitation to engage if I chose to; to listen if he was good enough, was moving.

My tears in that moment, though, also sprang from a reminder of my own sense of purpose; beginning, as I was, to work on this book. My passion has been to give voice to the stories of those who are seldom heard. In 1995 I brought out a book called *Found Wanting: Women, Christianity and Sexuality*[1] because I felt that church sexuality debates at that time were almost entirely focused on male homosexuality, and that human experience was much wider than that. My concern was to dislodge the rigid cage that I termed, 'the curse of complementarity', which underpinned (and still does) all aspects of the church's understandings of gender and sexuality, and had the effect of marginalising most women. Complementarity asserts that we find fullness of life in relationship with someone of the so-called 'opposite sex', which somehow makes us whole, and that this should be lived out in lifelong heterosexual marriage – the ideal life. Through the stories of women – single, married, partnered, mothers, lesbian, straight, clergy, lay, divorced, and survivors of abuse, the book explored the alienation and distress that many felt with the institutional church; the resulting ambivalence about embracing the identity, 'Christian', and the challenges and possibilities involved in continuing on a journey of faith as women of Christian heritage. *Found Wanting* was an attempt to carve out a creative space in the midst of an otherwise cacophonous, tedious, and one-dimensional debate about who we are, what we are worth and whether or not we can be allowed to belong.

Found Out is a different kind of book. My focus is on reconstruction, not critique. In the intervening twenty or more years, women have been getting on with living and loving; negotiating changing relationships; changes in our sexuality and sometimes our gender; finding a language to make sense of life, a language to speak of God and of our spirituality. These themes are what interest me.

Reflection

You wept in the fulcrum of unrest. You had re-entered hostile territory where you knew you would be at risk. Last time you were there they tried to stone you. And before you even reached Bethany, you were met by Martha, distraught and bewildered, having come from a home disrupted by the chaos of loss and grief.

Your tears transformed everything. At the tomb you called, in a loud voice, 'Lazarus, come out.' Everyone expected Lazarus to be a terrible rotting stench who would pollute everything he touched with his miserable corpse. Surely he should stay in his winding sheet, wrapped up and made safe in his cave behind a rock. But you said, 'unbind him and let him go'. So Lazarus was returned – a gift and a blessing, restored to his loving family, taking up his life with them. It was the opposite of what everyone understood and expected. He was not a reanimated corpse or a circus trick or unclean, but a totally new thing, born of love. But what must it have cost him? How many voyeurs would come to gawk, to doubt, to disbelieve?

And politically, Lazarus was now in danger, his resurrection the catalyst for murderous plans. As the chief priests and Pharisees said, if they were to let you go on like this, performing such astounding miracles, everyone would believe in you, and the Romans would threaten their power-base. In the interests of nationhood and their 'holy place', they plotted the expedient sacrifice of you – the one in whom liberation could have been found. So your tears wrought the transition into your time of Passion.

In exploring again this terrain of faith and sexuality and gender, I have found it difficult sometimes to hold myself open, and not to retreat into a world-weary hardness of heart. In those times it has been the contributors to this book who have enlarged me and given me hope. In particular, I have returned often to a meditation by Phoebe which I will quote in full now. She captures a vision of compassion and generosity in the midst of the pain and discomfort of debate. She was inspired to write this piece by Sara Miles' book, *Take This Bread*[(2)], and it is a precursor to much that follows about change, transformation, transition and liberation:

> 'It's all terribly inconvenient isn't it – all this thinking, searching, hungering – exhilarating, but exhausting, confusing, and scary…I wish I were wiser, I wish we were all wiser…(body, blood, bread, wine poured out freely, shared by all). So we gather, sit, share in long and complicated conversations, honest disagreements, trying our very hardest to be love-bathed and authentic, grappling, wrestling…(the most ordinary yet subversive practice: a dinner table where everyone is welcome, where the poor, the despised and the outcasts are honoured). We struggle with change, but ache for transformation, so we hope, persistently and passionately, that our gathering together – our drawing close – will stretch us somehow, widening what we think of as "community", relentlessly challenge our assumptions about religion, and politics, and meaning (we are more than grand promises and petty demands, temptations and hypocrisies, ugly history and insufferable adherents)…breaking us apart, then gracefully reassembling (food and bodies, transformed). Then here, maybe even here, we'll find ourselves winding up not in what people like to call "a community of believers" – which tends to be code for "a like-minded club" – but in something wilder, scarier, more mundane than we could ever imagine: the suffering, fractious, and unbounded body of Christ (fed with this ordinary yet mystical bread). This is still my belief: that at the heart of Christianity is a power that continues to speak to and transform us – a voice that can crack religious and political convictions open, that advocates for the least

(least qualified, least official, least likely), that upsets the established order and makes a joke of certainty. It proclaims against reason that the hungry will be fed, that those cast down will be raised up, that all things, including my own failures, are being made new. It offers food without exception to the worthy and unworthy, the screwed-up and pious, and then commands everyone to do the same. And it insists that by opening ourselves to strangers, the despised or frightening or unintelligible other, we will see more and more of the holy, since we are one body: Christ's. So we say, still say, and will continue to say, "Taste and see" (Christ's body, broken for you).'

We should be in no doubt that this really matters. As I set out to put together this book, I occasionally doubted the need for it. Is the battle for LGBTI equality not all but won (at least, everywhere but in church)? But then suddenly there erupted a global backlash against all the gains we might have thought were secure; a kind of resurgent nationalism based on insecurity not confidence, bringing in its wake a passive-aggressive machismo, deep sexism, and so-called homophobia. (Most people use the word homophobia when what I think they really mean is a violent assertion of heteronormativity. The latter term may be a mouthful, but I prefer it for very important reasons. Homophobia takes away the agency of the one who performs it. It suggests a feeling of fear that one cannot help – like arachnophobia of agoraphobia. Being verbally and physically abusive to, denying the life experience of, and questioning the integrity of those who have an affectional orientation to someone of their own gender *can* be helped. It is a conscious choice.)

And the lived reality of persecuted LGBT people in many parts of the world serves to underline the fact that protecting the rights we have gained, and continuing to work for those rights where they have not yet been granted, is a life and death undertaking. One of the contributors to this book is Asma, who identifies as a

Muslim with a lesbian identity. She is now living in the UK having been a refugee from an African country where being a lesbian is illegal, where there is strong societal discrimination against LGBT individuals, and where no LGBT organisations exist.

Growing up, Asma felt different. The way she felt inside was 'really, really different'. But she hardly ever saw anyone gay, and the only sexual orientation open to her was heterosexual. The thought of marrying a man was to her, 'the most horrible thing that they might put me through'.

Asma met a woman and fell in love. She found this amazing, 'Like someone is pounding something on your chest'. They connected in a heartfelt and fun way. 'Nothing really matters when she's there, everything is brilliant for me, I could carry on walking twenty-four hours without resting because she's there.'

But Asma was confronted first by her brother, then by the rest of her family. She was beaten. 'They slapped me, and if I say a slap, it's horrible, because, they're men, they're taller than me, I'm not built with strength, it feels like they're hitting me with rocks, it feels like they're hitting me with metal because they were angry and they weren't going easy. It was with force.'

'In the end, I had to cover my head and sit on the floor. So now they had to use their legs to kick me. I was kicked in my stomach, my ribs, my back. They stamped on my face. I was kicked in my neck, and that left me semi-conscious, so then I had to scream, "OK, OK, I'll do it". I had to agree to marry, just for them to stop, because it hurt. And the most painful bit was my mum. She just stood there, you know. She just stood there and watched.'

Let's return to where we began this chapter – with weeping. In her book, *Seeing Through Tears*, Judith Kay Nelson explores the notion of crying as a form of attachment behaviour. It is, she says, relational, not individual. Crying is a way to get close, and not just a vehicle for emotional expression or release. She says, 'We do not cry because we need to get rid of pain, but because we need connection with our caregivers – literal, internal, fantasised, or symbolic – in order to accept and heal from our pain and grief. Crying is not about what we let *out*, but about whom we let *in*.' (3) Later in the book she talks about 'transcendent' or 'spiritual' crying, which is the most mature level of crying in adulthood, 'These tears are about something other than personal loss or pain. They are tears that represent oneness and love, closing the circle of attachment and loss by returning to connection.' (4) As women we long to connect: with ourselves – to be in tune with and live out who we feel we really are; with others whom we love in diverse and glorious ways; and with our faith heritage – which often has to be redeemed for us and by us.

Story

She sat opposite me on the tube train, crying. Tears were running down her face, and she had no tissues. She seemed to be in so much pain, and was trying to suppress it. I had tissues in my bag, I knew it. I located them. Should I offer them? Should I ask if she was OK? Would it help, or would it makes things worse? I was getting off at the next stop. I needed to decide.

In that moment of indecision I began to remember. I remember sitting on a train out of the city, heading away, for the last time, from someone I loved – so deeply, but not straightforwardly. Loved, not as a lover, but as one crucial to my self-understanding, my creativity, my livelihood. Now gone. I was desolate. The tears ran down my face. The train was crowded, and I wanted so badly for nobody to notice me. I wanted to be with my sorrow in a private place. I wanted to be alone with my mixture of incomprehension, powerlessness and disbelief that this brutal separation was the only way.

And I remember Paddington station. Crouching, animal-like in a toilet cubicle, rocking with a pain so acute I could hardly breathe, having to suppress sobs because you don't sob uncontrollably in public places/toilets, even behind a closed door. It was a whirlwind argument with someone with whom I was deeply connected. Over a seemingly trivial thing, but it felt as though the connection was torn irreparably at its heart by angry words. Words uttered minutes before the departure of his train. We were ripped apart by the unavoidable finality of an external timetable, with no possibility of resolution. Would there be a reconnection? How and when? In that moment it felt like we were riven forever.

Because of my memories I wondered, what if this woman was just holding it together enough to make it to her destination? What if my empathy made that impossible? But what if she was desperate not just for tissues, but for a kind word, an act of compassion. Crying disrupts the order of things. I did nothing.

Tears are both purifying and transgressive. Chemically, they contain those things which would cause us harm: 'emotional tears evolved to eliminate certain chemicals from our bodies and to help restore our equilibrium after stress. The popular notion that it is good to "cry it out" takes on new meaning…if it turns out that tears are literally excreting the chemicals that our bodies secrete when we experience stress.'[5] Anthropologically speaking, though, tears are in the category of stuff that traverses the boundary between the internal and the external. When bodily fluids flow, they represent the threat of pollution. It's better that it doesn't happen in public.

That tears run through this book should be of no surprise. Many of us have transgressed boundaries and been considered abject when all we have done is attempt to embrace our identities as spiritual, sexual and gendered people; identities that go as deep as it's possible to go. Violation of who we understand ourselves to be is the deepest violation. People will become refugees, literally or metaphorically, because of it. So the tears here are sometimes the tears of separation – of distress, isolation, exclusion. But they are also the tears of connection – of joy and discovery, of solidarity, of finding new spiritual homes, and a life-affirming sense of God, the ultimate caregiver. They are the tears of purification as we set aside the distress of life as supplicants, saying 'please', and embrace our agency as prophets and pilgrims building something new. They are the tears of having been found out by the mercy and freedom of God, and the tears of having found out new directions, new habitations, and new forms of language. They are the tears of deep calling to deep.

Chapter Two

Retrospective

Reflection

You seemed to suggest that there is a divine force in the universe that ensures that 'the truth will out'; A gravitational pull behind everything, drawing what is buried to the surface. It may take years, decades, centuries or millennia, but it will happen. You talked a lot about burying things then digging them up again; losing things and finding them. And you said that nothing is hidden that will not be disclosed, nor is anything secret that will not become known. It was as though you were speaking of a simple inevitability. And why, you asked, would anyone want to hide a light that they have lit to illuminate the world? Who would want to do that? It makes no sense, for the purpose of light is to shine. The purpose of us is to be. Never learn to hide what's good.

But then you said something harder to grasp. 'Pay attention to how you listen'. Be careful how you listen to truths that are emerging from the shadows. When new things come to light about the world and its people, we have two choices: listen well – that is, listen and be changed – and we will be given more understanding. Or we can listen badly, or not at all – shoving the new insight into old categories of thought (putting new wine into old wine skins), forcing experience into dogma-shaped boxes, prioritising ideology over humanity. What then? In that case, even the little understanding we thought we had will be taken away.

'Hands up if you think homosexuality is wrong', said my history teacher. I didn't have to think. I kept my hand firmly down. To my shock, a majority of those in the class raised their hands, including my best friend.

'Now put up your hand up if you think there is nothing wrong with homosexuality', said Mrs Wilson. I put up my hand and found myself part of a small minority. I felt both defiant and exposed. It was comforting that those I agreed with were people I liked (at least one of whom subsequently turned out also to be gay), but it was confusing to be at odds with my best friend, with whom I shared everything. I was very clear about my opinion, but with little idea about why I held it. And I was just as clear that my friend was wrong about hers, with as little idea about her rationale.

This was my third year at secondary school. I was thirteen. It was 1979. This was a pivotal moment in my personal retrospective. It was memorable because it taught me something, though in the moment I didn't yet know what I was learning. I don't remember much about the classroom debate that followed the show of hands, though presumably there was one. But I remember that it worried me that my friend and I had ended up on opposite 'sides', and I reflected on this a lot in subsequent days.

I realised that my firmly held opinions were not really mine. I assumed the same was true for my friend. Our positions were two sides of the same coin, and the coin was the inherited thought processes of our families and our culture. My friend's family was more conventional than mine. Her dad worked from nine to five each day, and her mum was the homemaker. Clearly, as a clergy family, this was not possible for us. They had long family meals together in the evenings and would spend many hours in debate and discussion. I enjoyed joining in with these when I was visiting. Her dad loved to pretend to be very conservative, presumably to teach us how to hold our own in an argument. He and I disagreed about most things, but I never really believed his espoused views to be authentic. He was a deeply compassionate man. Whilst these interactions were mostly intellectual and abstract (and good natured), I remember a growing awareness that my opinions had ontological implications. At an intuitive level I knew that I would be 'different', and would not live as most people lived. More specifically, getting married and having a family were not what I aspired to, unlike my peers, and I knew this was not what counted as 'normal'.

This was probably the beginning of what has been an ongoing process of thinking and rethinking issues of sexuality and gender. I want to offer now a retrospective that spans from then until now, exploring other pivotal moments for me, and what I learned through them. I do this not because I consider my own experience to be in any way special, but because I believe it is not. When it comes to sexuality and gender, each of us has a retrospective that is personal. Each of these is impacted by wider cultural forces – family, economics, cultural mores, geo-political change. When we share our stories we begin to build a clearer sense of how things have changed, why other things have stayed the same. We create a shared understanding of how change happens, and therefore how change can be facilitated in the future.

That year, 1979, saw the beginning of the best part of two decades of Conservative rule. My political awareness was barely more than nascent, but I felt a deep sense of dread when Margaret Thatcher won the election. Temperamentally, I knew that things would be bad. As one already ill-disposed to rigidity and rules the thought of being governed by a hard-edged and overbearing matriarch with no apparent trace of compassion was not palatable.

And so it was that the next twenty years were, indeed, characterised by the indelible marks of an ideology that created unemployment, poverty, vicious racism and heteronormativity, militarism and gender-based violence. Now, looking back, I see the incident in Mrs Wilson's classroom as a stray thread in a garment of convention and hidden rules, which unravelled over the next couple of decades through a series of events that I experienced as – on one level – random and unrelated, but which at a visceral level

I somehow knew to be inextricably linked. To know how and why they were linked needed political and intellectual frameworks that I had not yet encountered or understood.

Jumping forward a few years, I am listening to the following words, 'I find it hard to address you as my brothers and sisters in Christ today, and this pains me.' This is my first experience of the annual Methodist Conference, my denomination's governing body. The speaker is Sybil Phoenix, a community worker in Lewisham and founder of the Marsha Phoenix Memorial Trust, a supported housing project for single homeless young women. She was the first Black woman in the UK to get an MBE (in 1973), an honour followed by the OBE in 2008. Sybil Phoenix had developed a programme known as MELRAW, Methodist Racism Awareness Workshops. I cannot remember what report or motion she was addressing, but it clearly had something to do with institutional racism, and Sybil was not impressed with the church's progress. I do remember my response very clearly, though. I felt desolate and had to leave the conference hall once she had finished her speech. I felt a deep sense of regret and personal responsibility. Even though I was only nineteen, and could think of nothing I had done personally to deserve being on the receiving end of her disappointment, I did feel that it was justified, and that this insight would and should change my life. I resolved that day to find out what I had done to hurt this woman, and others like her, and to figure out what I could do to undo what I (and others) had done.

So I learned that day that doing harm is a corporate thing. You may not choose it as an individual. Indeed, you may hate the fact that the harm is being perpetrated. But if you are part of the grouping (in this case White people) that has privilege without having to choose it, to the extent that you accept and do not question your entitlement to the power this gives, you are part of its misuse. You are a contributor and a colluder unless you consciously become a detractor. That felt like a huge realisation, and a life's work to know what to do with it.

I had encountered Sybil Phoenix a couple of years before, in a more intimate context, as a Methodist young person in International Youth Year (1984). My denomination took its young people extremely seriously. It gave us opportunities to travel the world, take responsibilities and learn leadership skills. Back then there was a famous annual event called the London Weekend, when 12,000 young people would come to the capital to take part in a festival, sleeping on church hall floors and attending events in theatres, Westminster Central Hall, and the Royal Albert Hall. It was decided that in 1984 young people should play a key role in leading the weekend. And somehow I got invited to co-host a discussion event called 'Speakeasy' for five or six hundred young people at Westminster Theatre. My co-leader was a young Black Methodist called Jeffers, and our mentor was a BBC Producer of religious programmes.

There were panellists whom Jeffers and I would interview – and the theme was Racism and Sexism. My interviewee was to be Paul Boateng, subsequently one of the first Black cabinet ministers under New Labour. Jeffers' interviewee was Sal Solo, lead singer of 1980s pop group Classix Nouveau. It was terrifying. But I remember most clearly the preparation leading up to it. We were put through a programme of awareness raising on the two themes that changed my life. And it was equally enlightening for both of us. Jeffers and I were booked onto a MELRAW workshop. As it happened, there was a mix-up and it turned out that since I was the only White person there, Sybil Phoenix ran a Black Consciousness workshop and I was allowed to sit in.

A young woman was recounting a workplace experience. She was a secretary and had made a mistake of some kind. Her boss (a White woman), had become frustrated with her and declared, 'That's the last time I employ a Black person.' Sybil asked how the woman felt about that. 'Well', she said, 'I can understand it. I mean, I had made a mistake and let her down. I can see why she would judge other Black people by my performance.' Sybil's gentle response was this:

'So tell me something. If a White woman had made that mistake, do you think your boss would have declared her intention never to employ a White person again?' I watched as an awareness dawned on the young woman, and felt it dawn within myself. Of course that would never happen. It was a ridiculous suggestion. I saw the penny drop, and I am sure that her life, like mine, was transformed by that insight. I remember how forcefully it came home to me, as the only White person in the room, how little I knew of experiences of racism, and how much my 'normality' was a White normality.

I gained an insight from that workshop that I have carried with me ever since – the difference between individual feelings and structural power. All of us carry a collection of what today would be called 'unconscious biases' based on past experiences – good and bad. These are our prejudices. I may say that I don't like cheese from a certain supermarket because I once bought some that was tasteless; or that I like gay men, because all those I have met have been kind to me. Racial prejudice is usually used to describe negative feelings of antagonism, and activities of discrimination against those from a different ethnic group. Any individual can be prejudiced against another, and discriminate against them, but the extent to which this makes a difference is dependent on how much power the discriminator has. In a society which is structured to favour one racial grouping over others (in the case of British society, to favour White people over minority ethnic groups), prejudice plus power results in racism of an institutional kind. And unpicking that is extremely complex, as was subsequently explored by the Macpherson report into the murder of the Black teenager Stephen Lawrence, exposing as it did the institutional racism within the Metropolitan Police.

What Sybil Phoenix taught us helped me make sense of the media stories of that time. Names of Black men and women were circulating – those who had died, been killed or been imprisoned, rightly or wrongly depending on who you chose to believe. Cynthia Jarrett died in 1985 when police searched her flat in Tottenham having arrested her son on charges for which he was later acquitted. She died in suspicious circumstances of a heart attack. A week later, police had shot and paralysed a Black woman, Cherry Groce, during a raid of her home in Brixton. Riots followed there, and there were subsequent riots in Peckham, in Toxteth and in Tottenham, where PC Keith Blakelock was killed during violent conflict on the Broadwater Farm Estate. Three men, most famously Winston Silcott, were charged with murder, although there were no witnesses and no forensic evidence. They were sentenced to life imprisonment, and not cleared until 1991.

The Tories blamed individual characters and attitudes for the riots, refusing to recognise structural injustices – economic deprivation and racism – as being at the root of the violence, right in line with Sybil Phoenix's schema. Disturbances and riots in major cities across the UK were related to racial tension and inner-city deprivation, and a distrust of the police and of the authorities: Brixton in London, Handsworth in Birmingham, Chapeltown in Leeds and Toxteth in Liverpool. The Scarman report that followed called for 'a direct co-ordinated attack on racial disadvantage' and proposed the formation of the Police Complaints Authority and the Police and Criminal Evidence Act. Whilst perceived to be riots between races, the disturbances were against White authority, state racism and the criminalisation of Black communities.

The Conservatives had instituted new powers for the police to stop and search people based on only a 'reasonable suspicion' that an offence had been committed. These so-called 'sus laws' were applied disproportionately to the Black community and were bitterly resented, especially by Black young men. A majority of the victims of the 'sus laws' were British born.

In 1973 Ann Dummett wrote *A Portrait of English Racism*[1], which was still a foundational text in our radical Christian household some fifteen years later (my recollection was that it was republished by CARAF, Christians Against Racism and Fascism, which was formed in 1978/9, in the late 1980s, but I cannot locate any evidence). Evangelical Christians for Racial Justice was founded in 1984, although those of us prejudiced against the 'E' word didn't immediately come within its orbit. Ann Dummett was head of the Runnymede Trust, the independent race equality think tank, from 1984 to 1987 and was a founder of the Joint Council for the Welfare of Immigrants. She showed how English society worked to define immigrants as 'others' and reinforced perceptions of difference, a prescient insight which has been borne out time and again in the decades since, and seems to be asserting itself ever more strongly today.

On the economic front, Monetarist policies caused high inflation (up to 18 per cent within the first few months of Thatcher's premiership) and in 1981 unemployment rose from 1.5 to 2.5 million in a year. Joblessness amongst minority ethnic people rose 82 per cent in the same period. In 1984 the National Coal Board announced a plan to close 20 coal mines – 20,000 jobs would be lost in many communities in the north of England, Scotland and Wales, which would therefore lose their primary source of income and identity. The miners' strike was iconic – a battle between the Trades Unions, and a Prime Minister who saw no purpose for them. Worse, she dubbed them 'the enemy within'. It was a test case, and she staked everything upon it, secretly stockpiling coal for months beforehand to ensure victory for the government. There was deep division, violence and unrest. In 1985 the Bishop of Durham, David Jenkins, expressed sympathy with the miners, and offered mild criticism of the government, saying simply that neither side should have total victory. He received vilification by the media, and apparently a long letter from the Energy Secretary who told him that as a Christian and as a Bishop, he was supposed to be on the Government's side.

David Jenkins was not the only Bishop to get into trouble at this time. After the Falklands War, the Archbishop of Canterbury, Robert Runcie faced down the Prime Minister's attempts to hold a triumphalist service of thanksgiving, insisting instead on remembering those killed on both sides, and emphasising the need for reconciliation. Meanwhile, mounting poverty brought forth other movements and initiatives from the Christian Community. Church Action on Poverty was founded in 1982, and when the Faith in the City report was published in 1985, political commentators began to refer jokingly to the Church of England as the 'unofficial opposition'. The foundation of the Church Urban Fund as a practical outworking of that report has ensured the investment of millions in community based anti-poverty initiatives in the UK for over twenty years.

As the Cold War threatened the 'Mutually Assured Destruction' of nuclear Armageddon, the Peace Movement was vocal, and Christians played their part. CND, founded in the 1950s, underwent a major revival, membership increasing from 4000 to 100,000 between 1979 and 1984. Bruce Kent, a leading figure in the organisation and a Catholic Priest, faced a government smear campaign dubbing him a Communist and a Soviet sympathiser. The Women's Peace Camp at Greenham Common airbase in Berkshire was founded in 1981, when people came to live outside the military base in order to witness and protest non-violently against the presence of nuclear weapons in Europe – then directed at the Soviet Union by the USA. Amongst the women, and the wider peace movement, were numerous Christians of all denominations and traditions. In 1982 30,000 women joined hands around the base, and in 1983 a human chain was formed stretching 14 miles from Greenham to Aldermaston, involving 70,000 people. The sight of women forsaking their domestic duties to live under plastic benders, cook on campfires, dance on silos and ululate in the middle of winters' nights, sent the Government and middle-England into a frenzy of rage born of incomprehension. Yet the creativity of the women's non-violent direct action, and their resilience and determination in the face of extreme opposition, including constant evictions, has influenced social movements around the world. The women claim to this day that they were part of a wider social movement which ultimately ended the Cold War.

My radical friends and I had been on many CND marches – protesting the apparent rush to Mutually Assured Destruction that the nuclear arms race seemed to be consigning us to. For me, though, the radicalising experience was a Saturday trip to Greenham Common with my well-meaning Christian Feminist Group from Moseley, Birmingham. I can't remember much about the how or when or what, but I do remember making sandwiches, and taking various things that we were told the women at the peace camp needed. Sitting round the campfire, chatting, I remember feeling something of a fraud. Here were women who were prepared to step outside of the confines of normality to live in discomfort because of what they believed in. And, more significantly, the reactions of the right wing press and Conservative politicians were vicious. These women, who were for the most part very ordinary, were demonised; accused of neglecting their husbands and their children, and even – imagine this – of being *lesbians*. Clearly the worst insult the tabloids could come up with at that time. The underlying hard-edged message was instructive. This was gender-transgression at its most threatening.

At around the same time, a man I had become friends with through Methodism's global youth empowerment programme came out to me as gay. It seems odd to me now that though I was in my late teens, he was the first person I was close to whom I knew to be gay. Given my earlier account of my surety of the goodness of gay sexuality, as evidenced in my history lesson at thirteen, you will no doubt expect that this did not faze me, but you would be wrong. It was very destabilising. My lack of confidence in knowing what to do with this disclosure, and how to be with him (did it make a difference? What kind of difference?), and the fact that his ministry at that time was pastoral care with young men working as sex workers in London, another whole new area of life for me, meant that if my demeanour with him was calm, then my emotions most certainly were not. It also pointed up for me the fact that I had not yet consciously reflected on my own sexuality.

The bigger picture is important here. In the early days of my university years (the mid 1980s) a strange word appeared in our College Chapel vocabulary, 'intincture'. This referred to the practice of dipping the wafer into the wine during Holy Communion in preference to sipping it from the chalice. The reason for this contested development was a new virus called HIV, said to be passed on through 'bodily fluids'. Little was known about it at that time, but the talk was that it was the cause of a deadly disease, called AIDS, with no known cure, and it seemed to be affecting gay men. For me, this was a terribly Oxbridge way to be introduced to a tragic disease with incalculable implications for millions of people.

The first recorded victims of HIV/AIDS were indeed gay, and the disease became associated in the media with gay and bisexual men. It subsequently became clear that this was nothing to do with their sexuality, but with particular forms of sexual practice which made heterosexual transmission also possible. Nevertheless, stigmatisation of gay sexuality increased. A sudden wave of hatred and scapegoating was unleashed. Rising negative sentiments towards homosexuality peaked in 1987. According to the British Social Attitudes Survey that year, 75 per cent of the population said that homosexual activity was 'always or mostly wrong', with just 11 per cent believing it to be 'never wrong'. Compare that with 2013, when the proportion thinking that homosexuality is always wrong was one third of that in 1987, whilst the 11 per cent who took the most relaxed view possible in 1987 had more than quadrupled to 47 per cent.

It is very hard to underestimate the impact that HIV/AIDS had on our society. Those of a conservative outlook, including Christians, deployed it as evidence of the punishment that lay in store for those who stepped outside the tramlines of what they deemed normal, respectable behaviour. The stigma was huge. Those too young to have lived through this need to know the extent and nature of the denigration experienced by those who were HIV+. And those of us who lived through it, but have also experienced the subsequent growing acceptance of so-called 'deviant lifestyles', and the scientific advances that have made HIV treatable and no longer a death sentence (at least for those in the world who can afford the medication), need to remember it.

What do I remember? I remember Simon Bailey, the first priest to die (in 1995) of an AIDS-related illness in the UK and to be open about it with his parishioners. He was the brother of a colleague, and subject of a BBC Everyman documentary entitled, 'Simon's Cross' and wrote a book called, *The Well Within: Parables for Living and Dying*.[2] I remember James Woodward editing his pioneering book *Embracing the Chaos: Theological Responses to AIDS*[3], an early pastoral response to HIV/AIDS. I remember in Ladbroke Grove, where I lived for a time, the Lighthouse Centre – a hospice for those dying of AIDS-related illnesses with a Christian foundation, offering unconditional love and acceptance of those who were HIV+ in a climate where many Christians were at best ambivalent, and at worst judgemental. And I remember that this was all highly contested. It was febrile, with talk of AIDS as God's judgement on gays and intravenous drug users, and the construction of those who contracted the virus other than through gay sexual activity as 'innocent sufferers'. The message to those of us coming to adulthood in the late 1980s was 'be normal or die, with only yourself to blame.'

And I remember the music and artistic creativity that exploded at the time. If you want to recall, or to understand, what was at stake back then, listen again to The Communards – whose albums became the sound track that ran throughout these years. Two songs in particular, 'Lovers and Friends' and 'For a Friend'. Both have a beautiful haunting, almost monastic, purity as they speak eloquently of love and loss, and the anger and contempt that is born of persecution. Blood families and faith 'families' were often the seat of rejection, so families of choice became crucial: 'Lovers and friends are all that matters'. Another hugely significant moment was the showing of the famous Names Quilt – a massive undertaking by the Names Project in San Francisco to create a physical memorial of those who had died with AIDS. The song by Sweet Honey in the Rock, the African American women's a cappella group (entitled 'Patchwork Quilt') says all that needs to be said. It is no coincidence, of course, that the other grouping most affected by HIV has been straight, poor, Black women. Sweet Honey remind us that there were men and women and mothers and fathers, sisters and brothers and daughters and sons, and children and babies and lovers and friends, all of whom had died with AIDS, now all sewn into one. When the Quilt was displayed, all the names were read out. As the song's refrain goes, 'And then they called out your name'. Hence the objectified and vilified were returned to their full humanity, echoing Isaiah 43, 'Fear not, for I have redeemed you; I have called you by name, you are mine.'

A new initiative was brewing on the British political scene that would recast debates about sexuality. The Greater London Council (GLC) began funding LGBT groups in the early to mid 1980s. In 1983 the *Daily Mail* reported that a copy of *Jenny Lives with Eric and Martin* (the story of a girl who lives with her dad and his male partner) was provided in a school library run by the Labour-controlled Inner London Education Authority (ILEA). Not surprisingly, Conservative political leaders were apoplectic at such developments, and were determined to stamp them out. The proposal was therefore to insert a new Clause into the Local Government Act. This 'Clause 28' (which became Section 28 when the legislation passed) said that a Local Authority shall not, 'intentionally promote homosexuality or publish material with the intention of promoting homosexuality'; or 'promote the teaching in any maintained school of the acceptability of homosexuality as a pretended family relationship'.

Section 28 became law on 24 May 1988. The campaign against it from the LGBT community (and others committed to free speech) had been fierce. Demonstrations were held on the eve of its passing, most famously involving lesbians abseiling into parliament, and another chaining herself to Sue Lawley's newsdesk during the six o'clock news, and being sat on by the presenter Nicholas Witchell – later the BBC's royal correspondent.

The only redeeming feature of Section 28 has been its unintended consequences. The most important of these, arguably, was the formation of the Stonewall Group. Ten gay men and ten lesbians came together to oppose 'the Clause' and to commit themselves to working with all political parties for equal rights for lesbians and gay men in all spheres of life. Some were famous (e.g. actors Ian McKellen and Michael Cashman) – some much less so. But over the last 30 years Stonewall has worked hard, alongside other lobby groups, towards equality in employment, recognition of civil partnerships, an equal age of consent, and equality in adoption, fostering, immigration and inheritance rights. Ian McKellen is now a 'Sir'; Angela Mason (Director of Stonewall for a large chunk of this period of change) has an OBE (for services to the lesbian and gay community), and Michael Cashman has been an MEP. It is no longer impossible to combine being 'out' as a gay or lesbian person with holding public office, and cultural attitudes towards same-sex relationships have shifted dramatically. Most young adults now see sexual diversity as simply a fact of life to be welcomed, not a moral dilemma to be solved.

In 1988, when controversy about 'Clause 28' was at its height, I was working for the Student Christian Movement. At the annual Congress Clause 28 was debated and, in the end, opposed. Students who considered 'homosexuality' to be sinful united with those for whom it was simply a gift from God, to oppose what they considered to be unjust and oppressive legislation. The debate was difficult and painful but the students recognised injustice when they saw it. As the person responsible for developing written resources for students, I worked at that time with half a dozen gay, lesbian and bisexual young people to produce a booklet called *Just Love*.[4] It was an imaginative collection, including engagement with the Bible and church history, but also stories, poetry and prayers.

Section 28 remained on the statute books until 2003. It was a nasty and stigmatising piece of legislation. Dismissing people's intimate personal relationships as 'pretended' was deeply insulting and unfair, and it was based on a misunderstanding about sexual identity formation which, though complex and little understood, certainly cannot be 'promoted'. Practically speaking, it hindered effective sex education in schools, and undermined attempts to deal with the very real problem of the bullying of gay and lesbian pupils.

In the 1990s there was a breakthrough in medical treatment of HIV/AIDs, growth in gay pride events and an increasing number of public figures coming out as gay or HIV positive. The age of consent was reduced to eighteen for gay men in 1994, and eventually equalised at sixteen in 2001. In 2004 the Civil Partnerships Act was passed, and in 2013 equal marriage. The campaign to end the ban on gays and lesbians in the military was successful in 1999; 2005 saw the launch of 'Education for All', tackling homophobia in schools, and from February 2015 (after some contestation and controversy) Stonewall launched its campaign for trans equality (having previously kept a strict distinction between sexual orientation and gender identity).

During the early 1990s, immediately after the introduction of Section 28, I worked full time for six years on issues of sexuality and gender. The organisation I worked with was called the Institute for the Study of Christianity and Sexuality (ISCS) and was founded in 1989 by Rowan Williams, Janet Morley and Canon Douglas Rhymes. Aligned with the Lesbian and Gay Christian Movement, the underlying philosophy was that no progress could be made for LGBT people within the church unless and until the sexuality of the majority heterosexual community was explored in depth, in such a way that people of all sexualities could come together to address themes in common. Because of the structural power inequalities between gay and straight, the emphasis was on the provision of safe spaces where everyone was considered equally loved by God. Nobody had to justify who they were to gain a place at the table. Our perspective was that in a world of inequality and oppression, differences between gay and straight were minor. There were bigger challenges to face, and deeper questions to ask, and these were better addressed together, all bringing our particular insights. We problematised the gender power imbalances implicit in heterosexual relationships, and the prevalence of sexual and domestic violence and abuse; explored the meanings of intimacy, faithfulness, celibacy and desire. We paid attention to how we might rethink masculinity, drawing on the thinking of James Nelson in the USA,[5] and Mark Pryce in the UK.[6] And we did all this by including gay and straight, men and women, and those from in-between places on these spectrums.

We learned that sexual abuse of children and adults was as common within the Christian community as it was outside of it, and that the denial that this could take place, and the silencing of survivors, was severe. We reached out beyond our shores to organisations in the USA that had made greater progress on these themes, bringing US theologians here to resource our own discussions and analysis. Mary Hunt and Diann Neu from the Washington DC based Women's Alliance for Theology Ethics and Ritual (WATER), and Marie Fortune from Seattle's Centre for the Prevention of Sexual and Domestic Violence (now the Faith Trust Institute).

Mary Hunt invited us to turn our thinking around by drawing a distinction between what is episodic and what is contextual. Societal structures encourage us to see violence and abuse as episodic – occasional, exceptional, that which is not often the case. Our majority context, we are persuaded, is one of sexual justice. Hunt argued that the opposite is in fact the case, and until we grasp that we will never make progress towards the eradication of sexual violence. She suggested that sexual abuse, across a wide spectrum, is the contextual backdrop against which we live as women, children and marginalised men. It ranges from sexist harassment in the workplace (back then widely regarded as 'harmless fun', but now recognised for what it is, a bullying abuse of power), to the systematic use of rape as a weapon of war and genocide. What is episodic is safety and peace; contexts where women and marginalised men can feel that they are not at risk from inappropriate words, touching, violation and exploitation.

We drew on the innovative thinking of Carol Adams who was making links between the exploitation of women, children and marginalised men, and the exploitation of animals and the natural world. Her book, *The Sexual Politics of Meat*[7] exposed the interplay between society's ingrained cultural misogyny and its obsession with meat and masculinity, and her *Ecofeminism and the Sacred*[8] was an early exploration of ecofeminism – a dynamic political theory that identifies how the oppressions of human and non-human creatures and the earth are interconnected.

Within the UK there was much creative feminist theological work underway, much of which seems to have been subsequently written out of history. In the wake of the consecration of the first tranche of women bishops in the Church of England, there was a brief explosion of interest in the press about whether this would herald bigger changes in theology and liturgical practice. More specifically, there was speculation about whether women in power might result in the use of female imagery for God. Whilst these speculations did not, as far as I know, originate from within the church, there was little comment from those in church leadership to put these speculations in a historical context. There was no explicit recognition that extensive work on themes such as models of God, divine imagery, critiques of exclusively male language for God, had been happening throughout the 1980s and 1990s. There was a time when no half-respectable clergyperson would be seen without a copy of Janet Morley's small slim green volume, *All Desires Known*[9] in their briefcase, alongside their Bible. And it was as though the St Hilda Community had not met and worked for years to develop imaginative, alternative, inclusive liturgy, as exemplified in their book, *Women Included*.[10] And that is just to mention one or two of the many and various resources developed and published in part to enable the churches to move towards ordaining women to the priesthood.

Evidence was emerging that children were being abused by supposedly respectable (and some very well known) clergy, including bishops; that clergy were operating in often dangerous ways, with lax boundaries, and little education or preparation about how to negotiate power relationships in ministry and how to manage their own sexuality in settings often highly charged psychologically and spiritually. We led retreats and conferences, lobbied for child protection policies and protocols (non-existent at that time); explored the potential oppressive effects of Christian teachings around forgiveness, the atonement (which was read by some as divine child abuse), teachings around the sanctity of marriage, the seal of the confessional, the unhelpful nature of seeing the church as 'family' where father knows best. We interrogated power differentials – spiritual, physical, emotional, and economic. We argued that churches need to be safer places.

Two stories in particular stand out for me from those years. Firstly, a regular at our conferences was a quiet and gentle man – very softly spoken, who one day spoke to me of his gender identity. He was a female to male transsexual (the terminology he used at the time). I asked him to write of his experience in our ISCS newsletter, and he did. This felt like the emergence of an extremely important 'new' area for exploration. At around the same time, a Methodist minister wrote to me of a pastoral situation she had in her church, where an elderly man had disclosed to her that he was a cross-dresser, and had come to the point where he could no longer keep this a secret from his wife. He wanted to give Joan (his name for himself when he was dressed as a woman) a less secretive existence. The minister was affirming and accepting of all aspects of her congregant's personality, was sensitive to the needs of the man's wife, but feeling a bit out of her depth as to whether or not she was doing all she could. She was seeking to learn from others who had encountered similar stories. There seemed to be so many areas of human sexuality that remained untouched by constructive ecclesial and theological engagement that we founded a new journal, *Theology and Sexuality* as a forum for developing new ideas and analysis. It continues to this day[11].

The question then is, what do these various moments in my retrospective amount to? I am one person, but I am a historically located person, and my life – like everyone's life – is a conduit for bigger social forces that weave themselves through my own story. On reflection, there are four key overarching themes which my experience points to as having shaped my generation.

Firstly, there was a sense that *Britain was considered great*. The greatest nation on earth. This came to the fore most markedly during the Falklands War when I was still at secondary school. Hysterical tabloid insults were thrown at 'the Argies' who were portrayed as good-for-nothing nobodies run by a 'tin pot dictatorship'. How *dare* they challenge our great nation? Who do they think they are? The possibility that Argentina might actually have a claim on the Malvinas (*their* name for the islands, which we therefore pointedly refused to use) was treated with disdain. The connection was made with gender when Thatcher sent off warships to defend 'our' territory. Triumphant nationalism was backed up by a masculinist militarism, with the first woman Prime Minister very much driving things. This seemed bizarre and self-contradictory to me, but I learned that women were not necessarily any different from men in the ways in which we deployed power, or in the causes for which we deployed it. Any romanticised notion that my soon-to-be feminist self might have developed, that the world would be a better place if women ran it, was snuffed out before it could gain life.

Secondly, *this 'Great Britain' was clearly a product of Colonialism*, and was aligned with White supremacism, underpinned by racism.

Whilst the phrase, 'the enemy within' was coined about the National Union of Mineworkers, it seemed clear to me that conservative world views divided 'the good' (those who accepted the rule of authority and got on with their quiet, conventional lives), from the 'subversives' (anyone who challenged 'normality'). Black people who challenged conventions which left them oppressed and disadvantaged were clearly enemies of the state, and it was suggested that they should 'go back to where they came from if they didn't like it here'. Running the country and being Black seemed an impossible combination in the 1980s.

Thirdly, *privilege and power were aligned with material wealth*. Having money made it easier to do what you wanted, have *what* you wanted, and have *who* you wanted. Thatcher unleashed a new kind of acquisitive Capitalism which has now infected and affected everything. A minority of the world's population are fortunate enough to be super-wealthy. Being indebted or impoverished or both is now the most common state for people on this earth. Human beings have been and are being commodified at an alarming rate, and this has made the trafficking, smuggling and sexual enslavement of people around the world ever more prolific. The thought that human beings could be bought and sold was far from eradicated with the abolition of the transatlantic slave trade in the nineteenth century.

Finally, there was a 'back to basics' way of life which in a common-sense way was deemed to be the wholesome building block of our 'civilisation'. The Christian churches were staunch and key promoters of this ideology. The nuclear family with a heterosexual couple at its heart was explicitly promoted as *the* ideal lifestyle. Aspiring to bigger and better things and greater levels of achievement was part of this: owning your own home; having a better job, and giving your kids the opportunities you hadn't had. In this compulsory heterosexuality, men were clearly in charge. Control was maintained through benevolence or, failing that, through violence (physical, verbal, psychological), or through sexual abuse. Rape within marriage did not become a crime until 1991.

Much has changed in my lifetime. But I would argue that the combination of colonialism and racism, male domination of public space and discourse, economic inequality and heteronormativity still impose a heavy burden on the lives of most people. We are currently experiencing a resurgence of racism and fear of 'the other' in the UK, along with a rise in anti-semitism and of a hatred of Islam (with the resulting gender contestations about what Muslim women should be 'allowed' to wear in public spaces). Similar forces are at work in the USA, where heteronormativity is also reasserting itself as LGBT rights are being freshly called into question. Oppressive forces are never vanquished, they simply re-form themselves and shape-shift into new manifestations. We have to learn to see them and recognise them, and pay attention to how we listen.

I have taken the time to try to describe how different strands of oppression interlock and combine. Consequently, a failure to address any of them is a failure to address all of them. Insofar as the Christian community finds it difficult to get its collective head around issues of sexuality and gender, its prophetic role in addressing the forces of economic inequality, neo-colonialism and racism, and the exploitation of the environment will be compromised too. Justice is indivisible. Sexuality and gender cannot be bracketed out and left to one side by a church that declares a key part of its mission to be 'challenging unjust structures'. The challenges before us remain huge, and making progress on gender and sexual justice is a necessary part of a much wider and all-encompassing task.

In the early stages of putting together this retrospective, I noticed a picture of a friend's daughter on Facebook. Chloe, aged twelve, had been photographed sitting in a pub, smartphone in hand, busy with social media, and she was wearing a hat with the slogan, 'Normal is Boring'. The image struck me as a brilliant summation of the contextual change that we have lived through, particularly in terms of forms of communication, where and how we get our information, and how we create interpersonal relationships. I wondered if I might use the image in a presentation I was putting together. I messaged her to ask permission, explaining a bit about the bigger project she would be part of (ultimately, this book). This was her response:

> 'Hey this is Chloe, I agree one hundred and ten per cent with your message, as I've found out there's lots of pressure on young people to act and be a certain way. For example, I often feel pressure to fit into a box and be who someone else wants me to be. As if someone is saying, "You are Chloe, you like pink, you are a cis white straight female and you will get an office job and get married and have kids", when I may not want that. I have a friend called Nathan and he is transgender and he's told me that he is constantly feeling pressure to wear dresses because his family doesn't accept the fact that he is a boy/guy and I believe that is because society tells people that he is not meant to be what he wants and is instead meant to become a part of what society accepts. It's the same for my friends Ali/Carl who is Gender-fluid. So I am more than delighted that you want to use an image of me to promote individuality and being yourself and not what other people think you should be... But yeah, that's just my opinion.'

I thought back to Mrs Wilson's history class. At Chloe's age I knew so much less than she about sexuality and gender. Even describing oneself as 'cis' (a person whose self-identity conforms with the gender that corresponds to their biological sex, i.e. not transgender) is something that would flummox and confuse most adults in our contemporary context, but it seems natural to her. The mention of transgender and gender-fluid friends, her natural embrace of the plurality of Ali/Carl's identity, and her drawing of parallels with her own experiences of constriction, restriction and potential rejection, astounded to me. And I have no reason to think that Chloe is atypical of her generation.

And yet still the predominant narrative is of pressure to be other than you are. The specifics may be different, but the forces of control are still at work. And they are at work in much more sophisticated and complex ways. There is evidence that social media is having a detrimental effect on the mental health of young people, because it imposes unrealistic and toxic lifestyle ideals from which it is hard to protect oneself, such is the ubiquity and fast-moving nature of new forms of communication. And neuroscience teaches us that the plasticity of our brains means that we have no idea how the adult brains of these young people will shape up.[12] Whatever the causes, there is an explosion of mental ill-health, eating disorders and self-harm amongst young people in our society, much of which goes untreated because of austerity cuts. How is their embodiment, and the mental health that is a consequence of it, being determined, and how deterministic will it be of their future? We also know that a high proportion of young people are gaining their knowledge of sex and sexual relationships through internet pornography. What will their relational lives look like in years to come, shaped by commercially-driven, computer-generated and enhanced, surreal images of such an important aspect of their humanity as their bodies and their sexual feelings?

Womanist practical theologian and psychotherapist, Phillis Sheppard, makes this argument, 'We need to consider "the body" in the context of a society where certain bodies are exploited to create a desire for commodities regardless of the need or ability to afford them; where the color of our skin continues to greatly influence our quality of life, our experiences of society, and our economic locations…where sex and sexuality are used to sell "entertainment" infused with violence. We need to hear what the body has to tell us about being created in the image of God.'[13]

Our young are, as ever, vulnerable to huge and multiple forms of exploitation. Many others are vulnerable too. Writing in her blog entitled 'Unstrangemind', autistic author, advocate and speaker Sparrow Rose Jones describes her struggles for survival, and the place of sexuality within it:

> 'Although I am so poor, I feel wealthy and fortunate because it is such a big step up from how I used to live. I have never been able to keep a job, which means before I started getting SSI [social security payments], I was unable to consistently keep a roof over my head or food to eat. I spent a lot of time sleeping in the park, in public restrooms, on loading docks. I ate at soup kitchens and out of dumpsters and off what food I could steal. I entered into sexual relationships with strangers in exchange for a place to sleep and food to eat. It's called survival sex and it was really easy for me because of my life-long training as a rag doll, compliant, always more concerned with what everyone else wants than what I want, feeling frustrated and worthless because, despite that strong urge to please I never could *actually* please anyone. So it was easy to give up my life, pitiful though it was, to someone else again and again and again in order to stay alive. My life was not worth much, but it was all I had and I clung to it. Survival sex means abuse. Survival sex means being asked to do shocking and disgusting things – not even all of them sexual so you probably can't even imagine the things I've been expected to do in order to survive. Survival sex means walking across the mile of bridge once again because someone thought it was funny to drive you out of town and drop you off alone, someone thought it was easier to deal with that slut they spent the night with by leaving her far away than risk that people they know might find out they were with her. Survival sex means risking your life, every day of your life, in order to stay alive.'[14]

Survival sex is probably as far from our promised 'fullness of life' as it is possible to be. Yet as a Christian community we are called to advocate for the latter, and to work towards it alongside others. The next two chapters explore how women have sought life abundant, for themselves and for others, often in the face of obstacles and obfuscations without which we could unleash amazing forces for good in this world of persistent injustice.

Chapter Three

Resistance

Reflection

The spectrum you had to negotiate was the one that runs from ecstatic affirmation to violent rejection. You elicited both extremes. Was this one reason you were an itinerant, constantly migrating from one place to another – choosing always to be on the road?

You modelled how to respond to acceptance and how to live with rejection, and you gave your followers a manifesto for both. When you sent seventy ahead of you, you told them how to play it. Set out with nothing; be vulnerable. But go in pairs, for solidarity. Enter a house, you said, and declare peace to the household. If the response was accepting, you said to stay, to accept what was given – food and drink and hospitality – and not to go elsewhere, but to use that place as a base for their activities, for bringing healing and liberation. If, on the other hand, the response was negative, you encouraged your followers to leave, shaking the dust from their feet – declaring why. You said it would be worse for those places than for Sodom.

Many were disturbed and threatened by your presence. Like the people in Legion's town. They were at a loss as to what to do with him – possessed as he was by many demons. Their solution was simply to tolerate him, naked and in distress, living beyond the boundaries of their town. When you came across him on your travels, you asked his name, then you healed him. You restored him to his full humanity – so he sat with you, clothed and in his right mind. But far from rejoicing at this outcome, the townspeople were gripped with terror at your power, at the change you had brought about. It was too much for them, and they begged you to go. You did not argue with them. You simply got in your boat and left but, leaving Legion behind, you encouraged him to tell his story. Most people like a comfortable place to stay, but those who face constant rejection are denied that luxury.

On another occasion, in Nazareth, response to you amongst your own townspeople went from adulation to furious antipathy within minutes. They thought you were speaking above your station, and they bitterly resented it. They rose up as one to drive you out but you seemed, somehow, just to pass through the murderous crowd and their anger, and disappear.

You suggested we should seek 'people of peace' where they are to be found, and that this would be in unpredictable and unexpected places. Why, you asked, do you look for the living amongst the dead? Why do you assume your allies will be amongst those who are supposed to love and accept you?

You put things very strongly when you urged us not to give what is sacred to the dogs, and not to cast our pearls before swine. If you do, you said, the swine will trample on them, and maul you. Who we are is sacred – a unique gift to the world, the treasure of great price. We know how it feels when that is trampled on. Your message is that we should get on with pursuing our calling to live out and pass on that gift, alongside those who would share in that: those who, by virtue of hearing the word of God and doing the will of God, become our siblings in God.

Tracey Byrne, Director of the Lesbian and Gay Christian Movement, reflecting during the aftermath of the terrorist attack on a gay nightclub in Orlando, Florida, in 2016, said this.

> 'The days and nights since…have been extraordinary. Whilst our church leaders' responses have been, almost universally,

grudging and inadequate, failing in some cases even to acknowledge that this was an attack which deliberately targeted LGBT people, in what should have been their safe space, the response of ordinary people has been quite extraordinary. Up and down the country, in our major cities and in our market towns, a spontaneous wave of love, compassion, ritual and remembrance has held people together and enabled them to express themselves in powerful, beautiful, hope-filled and authentic ways. In vigils and gatherings large and small, sometimes in places of worship, but often on street corners, in the market places Jesus would recognise, people have come together and somehow, instinctively, known what to do. These are dark days, but these images and your accounts of them on social media and as people contact the LGCM office, fill me with hope. Those of us who profess the Christian faith would recognise in all of this the movement of the Spirit, the first stirrings of resurrection. Our challenge now is to continue to stand together, to face up to and embrace what this is telling us about our world and about our church, and to organise for the road ahead.'

In this chapter we hear the stories of a diverse range of women – from all parts of the sexuality spectrum, single and partnered – all of whom are negotiating the complex terrain of how Christian teachings and assumptions impact on their identity and life choices. Juxtaposing these stories one with another helps us to build a picture of theological systems of silencing and control.

Living the Ideal

Anna

'My conclusion is that the church loves vanilla heterosexuality but those who seem to perform it have never actually performed it. People disclose extraordinary things to me as their parish priest and I can tell you that appearances are almost always deceptive. I have lived a life of messiness where God is found. The narrow vanilla understanding of human beings covers layers of silence. Trans, gay, all hidden for the sake of the institution. For a vicar, the internal silencing becomes increasingly crushing. Being partnered and gay, and unable to be public, leads to a ministry of loneliness and tremendous pressures. You are the holder of many other people's secrets, and then you have to hold your own secrets as well. Friendships are structured around church and a masculine ideal. There is the loneliness of not fitting the normative categories, and of not being able to say, "this is my lover". It is psychologically pernicious. Gay clergy get the crumbs from the table. Living as I do at the intersection of being a woman, lesbian, transgendered, disabled, and chronically ill, all these strands operate like electric cables – they are the conduit for power and creativity, but you can also end up getting electrocuted.'

Mary

'Everyone wants to be seen and known – to be accepted and valued for who they are and what they can bring – and while churches are sometimes wonderful at this (it is part of the calling of churches to embody the kind of community in which all are understood and engaged with as extra/ordinary human beings created in the beautiful, complex and mysterious image of God), this is not always the case.

As a mother of a toddler (and, incidentally or significantly, a priest in the Church of England) I find it hard to find spaces in churches to inhabit authentically. It is not that people aren't welcoming: congregations desperately want babies, children, toddlers, and young families. And in some ways, being a mother is exactly who the church wants me to be: the idealised maternal or nurturing figure (Mary rather than Mary Magdalene), and my sexuality and sexual expression contained within heterosexual marriage and used to procreate. So, why has it been hard to find a space to belong? I am not sure. Perhaps it is something to do with the fact that I am still trying to discover places where I can be simultaneously mother of a young child and a priest—and an academic, which is my day job. Most priestly jobs are full time and require a willingness to move to a parish: this is not possible if you are tied to living in a particular location because of a spouse's employment. Part-time jobs may still involve working hours (e.g. 5–9pm) that are very difficult with toddler bath and bedtimes and childcare pick-ups, and/or are "house-for-duty", which would again necessitate a move. So, maybe there is a need for dioceses and congregations to be more creative and proactive about posts which allow for more flexibility, and maybe even that allow for "alt-priests" – priests who inhabit multiple vocations or roles simultaneously? "Alt-ac" is a phrase that has emerged in academia to talk about those who are working as academics but not in traditional tenured faculty roles. To me, this would enhance and deepen our understandings of what it means to be a priest, rather than diminishing the role or calling – as it situates ordained priesthood within the priesthood of all believers and within the messiness and complexity of life. I hope that I still have much to offer as a priest – pastorally, liturgically, spiritually, sacramentally – and long to discover spaces in which I can do that as and out of being a mother (and an academic, and someone who lives to sing, run, and travel and bake…and… and…). Anecdotally, I have picked up that other Mum-priests have some of these struggles too—though I've never sat down with people and really talked about it. I sometimes wonder how many women the church (of England at least) has lost to active ministry (at least temporarily) for similar reasons to mine?

What is more, I'm not sure that we are very good in churches about engaging with the reality (as opposed to the ideal) of motherhood. I can only speak of my own experience. It has simultaneously been wonderful and hugely challenging to become a mother – involving a seismic shift in identity; complicated grief about a freedom and sense of youth I had before becoming a mother; delight and meaning in being a mother I had not dreamt possible; the sense of being pulled in multiple directions all the time, and a sense of failure that I am not giving enough to work, my son, social justice engagement, and so on; the tedium of a day involving playing with the same toys over and over again, changing nappies, cooking food; and the isolation paradoxically coupled with new friends; never mind the shifts in intimate relationship with my partner and shifting patterns of friendship and social life. Where are the sermons and discussion groups, and study resources, or prayer opportunities to explore or bring all of this? Where are there spaces for us to grapple with these changes, the delights and opportunities, moments of grace and sin, in relation to being a parent (and this I am sure applies to many fathers and other carers too)? Where can this complexity of experience be named honestly before God, and be lived with others in hopeful and at least attempting to be faithful community? I have a hunch that if we could create some of these spaces, church would become more attractive – at least for some.

I heard a discussion on the radio recently for Mothering Sunday, where some women were discussing how painful celebrations for Mothering Sunday were for many women—including those who are single, and those who have been unable to have children or who have lost children through miscarriage or stillbirth or later in life. They argued, very understandably and poignantly, that Mothering Sunday was excluding and made them feel wretched. I do not particularly connect with Mothering Sunday either, not because of this—but because it does not seem to engage with how messy and compromised this business of parenting is. So, I'm just left wondering, how are we managing as the church to make some with direct experience of mothering (like me, be that biological or adoptive) and some without direct (but perhaps much indirect) experience of mothering feel unseen and unheard—or at least unable to feel that they can bring their whole selves into church, and have a space in which they can grapple with their struggles before God and one another? Where are the spaces where we can just be ourselves, and share our struggles and delights of being a parent, single, divorced, married, widowed, gay, transgender, lesbian, straight, carer of adult parents or children, working in a day job while having other roles, and all the guilt and hope that accompany them? While I am not suggesting that the church needs to become psychotherapist or counsellor, could the church offer a space in which we can have more real, authentic conversations about what it means to be a complex human being—without feeling the need to hide behind expectations or that it is not acceptable to say certain things?'

*

In some ways Anna and Mary come from very different places in terms of their acceptability within the church. Anna brings together many strands of exclusion in who she is, and Mary many strands of inclusion. As Mary says, she is living out her procreative sexuality in a way the church considers to be ideal, yet she finds no space to be both a priest and a mother of a small child, and no contexts in which she can be honest about the reality of motherhood, with all its joys and challenges. Both women are struggling with dynamics that serve to silence them. Anna's term 'vanilla heterosexuality' points us to a plain, unexciting, non-threatening manifestation of sexuality that we are supposed to want – but in reality few people do want it, and even fewer have it. But the silencing creates a damaging and stressful form of secrecy about non-vanilla life and love, and it takes away places and spaces where simple realities can be honestly and openly explored and expressed.

What is being Resisted?

Vivienne

'I am part of a tradition, but growing up we felt outsiders in that tradition. The Christian community wanted to claim us, but my dad didn't feel comfortable being claimed. As a Black man who divorced, he experienced both racism and judgemental attitudes towards the ending of his marriage. So we made our own rules, which were very Bible-based. My dad knows the Bible really well.

My experience of religion is very experiential. For example, if we had no money for food, we'd pray about it. So my faith has served me in a really practical way. My gut and instinct says "do this", and I know that that is the way God speaks to me. My dad has always said that the church isn't always right.

I worked for a theatre company made up of born-again Christians. They were liberal enough to be in the arts, but were rigid on "no sex before marriage". They would say, "being a Christian means this", and "being a Christian means that", and I used to have really passionate arguments with them. It made me doubt myself. I felt, "Am I a bad Christian?", and "Can I really call myself a Christian?"

There were weekly prayer breakfasts. From being very young I had found praying very easy to do, but I always feel incredibly emotional when I do it, and very shy. I'd always cry. And these prayer breakfasts seemed to involve speaking in a special language, and I didn't know how to join in.

One of my friends from that time kept getting drunk and kissing other girls. Then she'd call me to talk it through with me, and I was really clear, "God has nothing but love for you". I suggested she might be a lesbian, but she kept denying it, saying, "I'm not, I'm not, I'm not. I can't believe God wants that for me." She was so sure, I thought perhaps I was wrong. As it happens, she's now married to a woman. Finding a church where she could be herself has been very hard for her. For a very long time she didn't go to church.'

Tessa

'As a chaplain in Higher Education, I have seen first-hand how difficult it is for young Christians to negotiate their faith and its perspectives on sexuality and gender at present. The greater cultural acceptance of LGBT identities and relationships has made it far harder for those struggling with faith and sexual orientation, as their struggles are now so much less well understood. It can be difficult for LGBT people to come out as Christian because Christians are so often the enemy. In therapy and support groups the church (and religion generally) is the oppressor and those wanting to hold onto faith and sexuality can think that impossible. That has always been an issue, but it's now more acute because of the churches being so far adrift from wider society.

Faith communities are now polarised over sexuality – both women's roles and homosexuality. I have been quite shocked to see how many bright students, including women, are willing to swallow agendas of male headship as part of a hardline "countercultural" religious identity. This applies to Christian Union students and Catholics (many of the Roman Catholic students are far more conservative on these issues than their chaplains) as well as other minority groups like Pentecostal and various free churches. Prior to my arrival there were also a few Anglo-Catholic students who would not have accepted a female chaplain, asserting themselves against the vote for women bishops in the Anglican Church and in solidarity with Roman Catholic students.

As regards homosexuality many Christian student groups pride themselves on a countercultural stance, at least at official and leadership level. I see a lot of students, particularly gay men, struggling with their faith and sexual identity. This is particularly tragic in the case of those clearly devout Christians probably called to religious leadership who for reasons of sex or sexual orientation find themselves excluded and second class citizens.

Another factor at work is globalisation. The development of an international anti-gay agenda fuelled by US Evangelical money and pastors, particularly in African Christian communities has exacerbated a latent cultural unease – the criminalisation of homosexuality in, for example, Uganda is a recent phenomenon, prompted by a hostile evangelical agenda. This has meant that within the chaplaincy the self-righteous homophobia of Christian Union members has been bolstered by the perception of students from countries with homophobic laws who could not understand the situation in the UK. This has created challenges in making the chaplaincy a genuinely inclusive place for all struggling with issues across the spectrum. For me, to adopt a solely liberal policy, inclusive of LGBT people (which one of my colleagues did) risks alienating the many students from non-UK backgrounds. I have made it clear that I am open to conversations with students across the spectrum and have sought to maintain the integrity of my own position whilst engaging with the fact that the churches (and faith communities generally) have a range of views. Conversations with some of the non-UK students have been very rewarding and enabled students to hear alternative views and consider other viewpoints and issues of human rights as well as different Biblical understandings. However, the fact that I as chaplain have to engage with a wide range of student views means that I am not generally out about my own sexuality as that would be a barrier, though where appropriate I might share a bit more of myself with individual students who are struggling.'

*

The question for many students, it seems, is who and what are they resisting? Is it the culture in which they find themselves which, for conservative Christians, has values directly at odds with their faith? Or is it their faith, which our culture perceives to be oppressive and excluding? Those seeking to offer spiritual support to students in the midst of this confusion face a complex balancing act – holding open a space where viewpoints and feelings from across a wide (international) spectrum can be honestly expressed, whilst also protecting those who are vulnerable – especially those who are LGBT – from hurtful interactions. What is true for young people remains true for all of us; we need to find ways to embrace the full complexity of our sexuality and relationships – and our personal journeys of identity, fluidity, and change should ideally be supported by faith communities that are flexible and responsive, encompassing challenges and questions. More often, however, as Vivienne's experience shows, nascent sexualities beyond the conventional are experienced as being tragically at odds with simplistic and rule-based forms of Christianity. This can mean, ultimately, that LGBT people (and those who are heterosexual and break the rules) end up having to choose between their faith and their sexuality. One way or the other, they end up in exile.

Obedience and Disobedience

Katherine

'I find it very difficult to think about my sexuality and faith because it's complicated. It's hard to talk about church because it's all wrapped up with my parents. Having to conform, having forms of behaviour imposed: this is how you behave, this is how you have to be in the world, because I was brought up in a clergy household. My parents weren't oppressive people, but there was much in my early childhood that I experienced as oppressive. It was *subtle*. No obvious gross abuse, but very subtle conditions surrounding everything. I am now very sensitive to those subtle forms of control. I don't know how much that was linked to church, and how much was just my parents. I remember my brother and I being introduced by them to various bigwigs, as though we were on display. I hated that. And I grew up with my parents having a conservative attitude to homosexuality, but I am not clear how much of that was a reflection of their theology.

Because my partner is an Anglican clergyperson, there is an expectation on us to be celibate. This is deeply painful because we want a relationship where we can be fully ourselves, including our sexual selves. To expect us to be celibate is ridiculous and, frankly, cruel. Until that changes, I will always be carrying something large, angry and bitter, and I will continue to feel very negative about church.

The fact that we are here, openly in a civil partnership, and my partner is operating in a traditional rural context, is positive, but only when compared with the past. And I don't think it's generally known that this is what is demanded of gay and lesbian couples by the authorities. I think it should be publicly known.

My anger and bitterness are very separate from faith and God. Church is just a flawed human institution. I've always been clear about that. God is much bigger, and in a completely different realm. The church hasn't got in the way of my relationship with God, and I'm glad about that.

I don't get angry with God about this issue. I find God in church in music, and maybe in the beauty of the building. But that's it. Not in the liturgy. And I find God in music outside of church too.

A lot of time I don't feel like I have a close personal relationship with God. I'm not sure I have a concept of God at all. But there is an expectation that I should have, and that prayer should be about talking, in words, to God.

My faith has deepened through the process I've been through with my partner, as she has gone through selection and training. We have quite similar views on things, and a similar make-up and sensibilities (apart from our approach to the sacraments), so we have talked a lot about these things.

As much as I have negative feelings about church, and feel that being ordained brings challenges, I have always seen what my partner brings to the role. It feels like part of my vocation is to support her in hers. I support her not because of what she is doing for the church, but because of what she is doing as a person of faith who gets alongside people where they are. There are some parallels with my own profession as a doctor, in which I have stepped outside narrow medical worldviews. I see many colleagues operating within rigid systems and ways of thinking, preferring to stick with boxes and labels. My partner and I have that in common. We are both "misfits" in our exploring of alternative ways of practising and thinking. We both know the risks of that, of not toeing the line, and knowing the dangers of crossing lines.

In some ways I do feel that I have responded to my partner's process in a supportive way, because I've experienced a similar process with my own profession. I know the territory. It's familiar. So perhaps I don't notice that it's a struggle. It's like chronic pain. You get used to it, you put up with it. Perhaps I tolerate it more than I should, because I can?'

Rebecca

'My partner talked to me about being transgender over ten years ago now. I had been exploring ordination for five years, and was going through the selection process. My Bishops' Advisory Panel (BAP) was scheduled for just after her diagnosis. My bishop's response to my spouse being transgender was to declare, "You can't go to the BAP, and you will never go forward for ordination. But if you get divorced, it won't be a problem". This was devastating to me. My identity as someone who was becoming a priest was completely and suddenly stripped from me. I had a meeting with the same bishop many years later, before he retired, as a way of gaining some closure for myself. But he just said, "You have annulled your marriage by your actions". By "my actions" he meant not leaving my partner. By staying loyal to her as she transitioned, I had apparently betrayed my marriage vows. There was, therefore, no resolution. For him, divorce was more desirable than being married to a transgender woman. I'd done nothing wrong. I had just tried to be faithful.

My experience of the families and partners of trans people is that we feel that we have to act as stabilisers for everybody. As supporters of trans people in the Christian community you are either idealised or you are wrong, and you just have to cope with it. Everyone has their own needs or expectations of the partner, both in the church and in the Health Service, but nobody thinks of the partner's needs. It is very isolating, standing against a massive tidal wave, alone.'

*

Obedience and disobedience are tricky concepts in a context where there appears to be no logic. There was a time when the church said that if only there was a structure within which gay and lesbian people could live in permanent, faithful and stable relationships, the church would support them. But once civil partnerships were introduced, providing just such a structure, there was considerable back-tracking and contestation about whether or not they should be endorsed. Nevertheless, clergy are not barred from entering civil partnerships. But these are, by definition, a promise to live in a mutually supportive, sexually monogamous relationship for life – just like a civil marriage. Yet Katherine and her partner are called upon to live a celibate life. What then, is obedience? Is it to honour the mutual promise made to one another, or to acquiesce in an external demand placed upon you by an institution for politically pragmatic reasons? Likewise for Rebecca, in a church that has always stood by the permanence and sanctity of marriage, to the extent that divorce is still far from acceptable, she is called upon to embrace a divorce she does not want in order to be acceptable for ordination.

Living with Restrictions

Tessa

'The Church of England particularly is very good at maintaining official positions, for example, accepting women priests, and clergy in civil partnerships, but in practice blocking by the back door those whose faces don't fit.

In recent years all those who have left the Diocese in which I was ordained without a post-curacy incumbency have been single women. On one occasion the Bishop made it clear that they would ensure that couples with kids would be found a parish – inevitably leaving those who were single and without a nuclear family in a far more vulnerable position. This is quite disgraceful discrimination and ignores the fact that single people have other family obligations. Care for my mum, though she is not strictly a dependent, is a significant concern for me; she will be eighty next year and has significant health issues caused by arthritis. Though I now live in London, part of the reason for accepting my current job outside the church is that it takes me back to the north-west moderately regularly so I can see more of her.

If you are single, significant others do not travel with you so your support networks can be decimated when you move. And the nature of clergy jobs, with non-standard hours and days off, makes developing those networks hard. On top of that, finding a partner is also more difficult; you are more likely to be single as a clergyperson if you are a woman than if you are a man. Being the curate's or vicar's wife is very different from being the spouse of a female clergyperson, and I know more single female clergy than male who are divorced. Three of my contemporaries from theological college became single when husbands left because they did not want to be a clergy spouse. For those of us who are LGBT, meeting a partner is even harder than for someone who is straight because that relationship is likely to have to be covert in a way that is no longer the case for those who are LGBT in the wider community. In some ways the progress of the rest of society has made the situation worse for LGBT clergy; I have watched lay LGBT Christian friends pledge love to each other whilst having myself been left single. I split up from the partner I used to be with as part of the process of going forward to ordination.'

Esther

'I moved to Cambridge in 1996 for work, and went to King's College chapel. I was bowled over. As a musician, I loved it. Not long after that, my mum died. I found that I needed both the silence and the music of the Chapel to make sense of that loss. I spoke to the chaplain at work (a hospital) at the time, about if there is a God, what role can God play. I found God in silence and the healing effect of music. I felt a calling, and finally decided to respond to it (it was ridiculous really, as I wasn't even baptised). But I was taken seriously by a vocations adviser.

Because I am gay, I had to have special permission from the Bishop to go forward for ordination selection. I was asked to live by 'Issues in Human Sexuality', and I said I would, though I have made it clear that I am not *happy* to live by it. I am *prepared* to live by it. There's a big difference. I feel it's not fair because it asks something of my partner that should not be asked of her. I have been totally open about my sexuality all the way through. I was in a civil partnership from before I went forward for ordination.

Here, where I have just begun my curacy, there have been very few rejections. And in the past, at previous churches where I've been a member, there have been people who were against me, and others who changed their minds. It has meant that finding a curacy in a rural diocese has been harder for me than had I been straight. But I think that will change in another ten years or so.

My faith had developed despite the church. The church is still trying to shape people rather than people shaping the church. The church is behind in this.'

*

In very many ways being a lesbian clergyperson is a no-win situation. If you have a partner and are open about it, you are a focus for dissent and controversy within congregations, or you function as a 'test case', the one that is talked about and weighed in the balance. Tessa becomes and remains single because of the disproportionate pressures and restrictions placed on lesbian partners. All lesbian clergy have their relational lives restricted and

Becoming Acceptable?

Janet

When you've been abused, you take away a sense of God from yourself. You pull away. It's about shame. When I was abused by a stranger as a child, I started being a boy because my dad couldn't cope with what had happened to me. He thought it was his fault because he had failed to protect me as a little girl. I thought my dad would find it easier if I was a boy. You feel there's something in you that's not right, and it's very hard to shift that.

I made myself invisible, finding acceptance of who I am in who I experience God to be. My vicar was critical of me. He said it was my fault. I thought of myself as unlovable by God. I was with two other girls at the time. They left me with the abuser and I was completely out of my depth. The only people that didn't blame me were the police.

It wasn't until I did a thirty-day retreat, and had an intense experience of God's love, that things shifted in a significant way. But then you have to go back into the world, and you start picking up all the signals again that you are not OK. That's why I find the Examen so helpful as my spiritual practice. Every day I play back the day and ask myself, where did I see God's love at work?

I wonder what would I have been if the abuse hadn't happened?

When I was training (to be ordained), I almost had a breakdown. My tutor suggested counselling. My counsellor pointed out that I had taken everything upon myself.

If something's not acceptable, you try to make it acceptable.

But everything that has happened to me is integral to my calling – it's an important part of who I am. Every time I have gone back to God in prayer, the same message has come back to me, "You're a priest".

But I still feel that the church isn't somewhere I feel comfortable talking about this. I have preached and spoken about it, but it is still somehow shameful.

Shame can be an important societal control, but it's what it's used for that matters. Shame draws you into yourself and won't be forgotten. Guilt can make you look out towards others, to do something different, but shame means that you're not OK, so you are always thinking from your own point of view. It stops you engaging with others and with God. Only God's love can change shame.'

Hannah

'As an autistic woman, I feel both medicalised and demonised. Expressions of gender and sexuality are different within the autism community. A much higher percentage identify as LGBT. I myself identify as a lesbian, though I am happily married to a man. Autistic people are being forced to conform to certain behavioural standards through forms of therapy known as ABA/PBS (Applied Behaviour Analysis/Positive Behavioural Support). These take away everything you value, and all that you are, so that you can then be socially reprogrammed through a system of rewards for behaving in particular ways that are convenient for those around you. There is a huge move against such therapies, especially in the USA, with some taking to the blogosphere to describe the effect these therapies have had on them, and the negative impact on their gender and sexuality, amongst other things. For example, in unstrangemind's blog, the author speaks directly to the parents of autistic children who may be seeking such therapies:

> "Children like yours – children like I was – are taught to be compliant. That's what 90% of autism therapy looks like to me: compliance training. They become hungry for those words of praise, those 'good girls,' the M&Ms or stickers or other tokens you use to reward them. They learn quickly that when

they do what you want them to do, they are a 'good girl' and when they try to do what they want, they are a 'bad girl.' I was not allowed to refuse to hug the man who sexually molested me for a decade of my childhood because I might 'hurt his feelings.' That's pretty major, but there were millions of minor experiences along the way, chipping off my understanding of myself as something owned by myself and not something owed to the world around me.

Even something so seemingly simple as the constant pressure to smile. Everybody wanted me to smile. And I was told that I was such a pretty girl and ought to smile. And I was told that I was so pretty when I smiled. And it was so important to everyone that, after a while, I sat in front of the bathroom mirror practising faces, trying to find the muscle-feeling that would make a smile. I practiced and perfected until I could make a smile on demand. I worked hard until I had a smile that made everyone happy and got them to quit bothering me. And now, when I am afraid that I am being a bad girl, when I am resisting what someone else wants, when I am feeling the pressure to be a rag doll again, to be whatever and whomever I am being asked to be, I put on that smile as a shield to protect the tiny scraps that are left inside me as I give in and give up who and what I am because the pressure to comply is so huge and so uncomfortable. And because I was never allowed to say no, never allowed to own myself, never allowed to not-want and still be a good-girl."'

Amanda

'I wanted to tell you how positive my visit to the USA is proving. The Episcopal Church (TEC) is so affirming and it is wonderful to meet gay married priests who are so open. It feels very free for me and so different from other visits. What a prophetic role TEC has and how they are persecuted for it. I have been telling them about

LEFT (Lesbians Exploring Faith Together) and my part in it in a way I wouldn't dare in the Church of England. It makes me realise what compromises I make with my own identity in other places. That's not bad necessarily but it does have a cost. It's the nature of the tightrope. It's like living with chronic pain. You get so that you don't notice it. It's the backdrop of your life. Then occasionally it lifts and you realise how wonderful life would be if it were no longer there.'

*

Learning to smile so that you can be perceived as a 'good girl' was a literal reality for the author of the blog, and it was instrumental in her sexual exploitation. But it could also be seen as symbolic of the many and diverse ways in which women are required to make ourselves acceptable; by knowing just how far to go in being open about ourselves, but not so far that others may know enough to decide to reject us. To 'become a boy' to save your father from his feelings of inadequacy in the wake of your abuse may be a logical solution for a child, especially one who is made to feel that what happened to her is her own fault. But Amanda poses the question – how would it feel if we didn't have to do any of this any more? If the chronic pain of self-censorship and of a strictly controlled regime of self-presentation were lifted?

Promises and Betrayals

Sally

'I grew up with a conservative understanding of sexuality. It became rather two dimensional, even cynical over time, though. You wait, and God sends you a good man, and if you are lucky you may be able to share in his ministry. But there just didn't seem to be that many candidates. A friend of mine said of Christian men, "they are too young, too wet or too married".

After a long time, I realised I was living my life on a temporary setting. In my mid-thirties I had a breast cancer scare. Getting the all-clear coincided with me feeling on the shelf and past-it. I realised I was keeping my hair long in case a prospective husband might like it that way. I was holding back. I needed this to change.

In 2004 I went to Central Asia. It was liberating not to have to get anyone's permission. I didn't need to. When I came home, I had a strong sense of the positive aspects of there being "nobody to meet me at the airport". You can look at that in a negative way or a positive way. I realised I was called to mission in this country. When I got back, I got a dog. Again, because I could. Because I didn't need anyone else's permission.

By Easter 2005 I had started going to my local parish church. There was a TV series back then called "The Monastery". Watching that, I felt the need to start again. I felt that the spirituality that had got me this far had done so only by the skin of its teeth. I was beginning to explore a more contemplative spirituality – away from the evangelical and charismatic. Focusing on my own sufficiency, and God's sufficiency. I began to have an inkling that having worked on chastity, celibacy might be the spiritual expression of that for me. I believe that chastity is what God expects of everybody. Celibacy is the gift of my chastity back to God.

In order to make sense of this I had to dig into the monastic tradition, which inevitably took me into the more catholic end of the theological spectrum. By the end of that summer I had decided that my calling was to lifelong singleness. It was akin to "coming out". I wanted to tell people that this was my understanding of myself and my vocation.

I was challenged by a church warden to celebrate it – to make a promise. An idea began to form that I would wait until my birthday in 2006, because my birthday had always been miserable for me: marking another year in which I had failed (to find a husband). In 2006 it was also Ascension Day, which seemed appropriate. I also felt it would be a good thing to couch it in a renewal of Baptismal vows.

The service itself was secret because I was under a lot of pressure from my family to get married and have children. Also, I didn't want any other women to think I was modelling for anyone else that this is the way to deal with being single. I wasn't. And in the midst of all that, I bought a house, which is a big thing for a single woman.

I told my story as part of the service, and I shared three scriptures that had shaped my journey over the years. Firstly, John 21, where Peter is reinstated by Jesus, and instructed to "feed my sheep"; then the words to John in Luke 1, "and you my child shall be called the prophet of the most high", and finally, Jesus' words in Matthew 19 where he says that some will be single for the kingdom's sake". Working with my parish priest, I wrote vows that captured all that for me, and I also used Psalm 62 which talks of God alone as my hope, my rock, my salvation and my fortress.

It's hard to articulate what this means, even in the Christian world. Offering for ordination was much easier as a result of having made the commitment. But on my three-day Bishop's Advisory Panel (the main selection event that gets you through to ordination), it's all they wanted to talk about. Married people didn't get questioned in such depth about their own sexuality and their relational decisions. I was in a place by then of feeling, "If this isn't what God is calling me to, I'll be bitterly disappointed." But being single and ordained, I realised I was going to spend the rest of my days in some way "suspect" in other people's eyes. It's as though I've got something to hide. I feel as though I've passed into being of a third gender. There is a phrase, "collar blind", that if you wear a clerical collar, nobody really sees your face. All I've done is that I've declined to participate in one of society's conventional institutions.'

Naomi

'At the age of 29 I entered a Religious Community with the intention of living a vowed life of poverty, chastity and obedience. During this time I was sexually abused by a Sister. The impact of this experience was devastating and I felt unable to speak, incapable of disclosing what had happened to me. I was silent.

It is doubly disenfranchising being an adult survivor of Clergy Perpetrated Sexual Abuse (CPSA) and a woman within the inherited church. Our "otherness" and being spoken for and about, rather than listened to, has enabled our experiences, as women and survivors, to be misnamed, denied and used against us. There is no specific guidance or code of practice addressing the disclosure of and response to adult sexual abuse perpetrated by clergy, ministers and religious. Abuse by "clergy" adds another dimension to abuse victims' experience: the spiritual dimension in which the sacred is violated. This cannot be quantified and is, by its nature, purely subjective. I define spirituality as, most simply as "a search for the sacred".

Reflecting on my own situation I was struck by the fact that silence is an integral part of my inherited religious practice – the "sacred" silence of inner contemplative prayer. It is an aspect of the Christian faith tradition which can be traced back throughout its history as women and men have desired a closer relationship with God. I refer to the violation of internal sacred silence as "Soul Violation".

Historically within Christianity there is another silence, a complicit silence of denial and self/institutional preservation. This has been particularly evident in recent years in relation to sexual abuse perpetrated by clergy and religious men and women and the response, or lack of it, by the institutional church. I call this "profane" silence.

In 1992 after a period of discernment I joined a Religious Community. I reached a point in my life where I wanted God and prayer to be the centrality and focus of my life. After an initial period of living with the Sisters as a Postulant, I was clothed as a Novice and received the Community's distinct habit of a full-length robe, a scapula and veil.

Joining the Community, the Convent became my home and I lived with some twenty women at various stages of their religious life. Life within a traditional Religious Community is deliberately boundaried in its scope and focus. Contact with others is limited. We ate together, with most meals taken in silence, and prayed together. The Divine Office punctuated our daily life and outside of chapel we strove to maintain levels of silence; the Greater Silence during the night and the Lesser Silence during the day when we were working. These external silences I refer to as sacred silence observed to help keep focused upon God.

From the beginning the Sisters were aware I was a survivor of childhood sexual abuse (CSA). Reverend Mother (RM) was supportive of my continued contact with Christian Survivors of Sexual Abuse (CSSA) and during my Novitiate I was enabled to set up a local 'Survivors for Survivors' CSSA group; a proactive response to my past experiences. Although challenged by religious formation, as most Novices are, I was certain of my decision to join the Community, and I was content.

Reverend Mother always stressed our rooms were not to be entered by another person except in extremis, illness counted as extremis. I was ill, and on one particular day AP (Abuse Perpetrator) came into my room and told me, "God wouldn't want you to be frigid..." and she abused me. I was effectively silenced by the abuse both in relation to God and those around me. From this moment on I felt too hideous to sit in silence or prayer to God. The daily Eucharist (Holy Communion) is at the heart of the Community's life and devotion. One day AP brought a piece of consecrated host (bread) from the Eucharist to my room and gave it to me. She brought this sacrament, "an outward and visible sign of an inward and spiritual grace", into the room where she was abusing me. There was collision of the sacred and profane and the sacred was profaned.

I name this devastation "Soul Violation" but struggle effectively to communicate what it truly means for me even though it affects all aspects of my life; the essence of who I am and who I am called to be before God. With sexual abuse there is a violation of personal boundaries: physical, sexual, emotional and spiritual.

As my relationship with AP changed I felt caught out and confused. As it moved from a mutual one of friendship it was really difficult to know how to describe it. I wonder now if my fears were used against me. AP knew about my history of sexual abuse and I suspect she used the information to construct a narrative to manipulate me. I also responded to her position as a Life Professed Sister within the Community. I was caught up in thinking "this person is caring for me" and therefore I reasoned she must like me but her actions left me thinking "what does this say about me?" It was a repetition for me of a past experience; a carer becoming an abuser.

I had actually liked AP; she was an important person in my life before all this happened. I trusted her. I believed she was a good person, so in trying to understand and explain I reasoned it was my fault I was abused; there must be something wrong with me because this is a good person who is liked. And if I told anybody they wouldn't believe me, they would see me as a "bad" person and not her, so it must be my fault.

If I speak about the abuse I feel ashamed…so I censor myself and I expect people to disbelieve me. I feel pretty damned. There is something quite hideous about being told God doesn't want you to be as you are, as if it is such a bad thing, because I have nowhere to go with it.

The emotional impact of the church's response spills over into the spiritual. This causes a tension for me particularly as the central point of the Eucharist is anamnesis; a call to recall God's benevolence and saving acts throughout history. It is a tradition built upon remembering. I am presented with a double standard to maintain the pious narrative of suffering.

This has not been an easy journey and it is only recently I have reached the deepest layer; being told "God wouldn't want you to be frigid" is, I realise, at the heart of my silence and distress. I was effectively silenced by the abuse and my abuser, both in relation to God and those around me. AP had used God as a theological justification for her actions – an extremely powerful position. Because of the impact of the abuse I experienced in my earlier life and how it impacted upon me, I felt deep, deep shame in front of God when AP said this. Soul Violation has the effect of silencing me in prayer. Shame, guilt and fear disrupt my relationship with God and add another, often hidden, painful dynamic of my silence.'

*

There is much in faith that is about vows and promises, keeping them and breaking them. For Sally, her vow to live as a single person was liberating. It was entered into freely and as a result of a sense of vocation and calling. It was a sign of a new understanding of her identity and an exciting process of fully embracing all that it meant. And so with Naomi's entering into the religious life, freely giving herself wholly to God – her whole self as a sexual and embodied person. How devastating, excruciating and bewildering that this vowed life was violated by one of the women whose role was to protect the calling, and to encourage and enable other women in their pursuit of it.

Objectification

Billie

'Coming from the NHS, which is by no means perfect – though it does try to put policies and good practice in place - ministering within the Church of England was like stepping back thirty years. Here are some examples of things that have been said to me:
 "Are you the lady vicar?"
 "What do we call you?"
 "Are you a *priestess?*"
 "You need to man up!"
 "Best to put up and shut up." (Regarding serious misconduct.)

"We had *hoped for* a nice married man with children…but we got you."

As I said, it is like going back thirty years. My children (aged twenty seven, twenty six and twenty three, who were brought up Roman Catholic and went to the local comprehensive school) would not dream of using such language, and are appalled by some of the attitudes they have heard in the Church. I think younger priests (under forty) tend to behave better, but perhaps the structure of the Church allows attitudes to become entrenched and unchallenged.

During the last few years, I have had uninvited approaches – physical ones, and verbal ones from priests. They are generally nice people – hugely respected and loved, and trusted by people and Bishop alike. I did not report any of this for several reasons: on one occasion, the priest was utterly mortified. He realised what he had done was wrong. He even 'phoned and said so. He was so upset, I found myself reassuring him. He was especially loved and embedded in the life of the church. His wife had even been present I think. Could all these things be reported? I judged not. I have also had unwanted things said (very suggestive, explicit things in my ear, during a church service, by a priest). I did not believe what I was hearing.

Then there are all the questions about my family life, "Are your children *with* you?" Of course people are curious, and that's acceptable – and actually, I don't mind frank questions, as long as people are respectful. Too often we can be superficial in conversation and "chat" and dealing with "spiritual things", theology and life, it's OK to be more serious, but cumulatively it has been painful (a year now, and people have posed the question very frequently: "are they actually *with* you?"). Local clergy have asked this too with, "We were wondering…." So one knows this has been discussed.

The fact is, they are adults and just on the threshold of leaving home: the youngest two coming and going as they have been at University. And yes, they always have lived with me (as a single parent since they were ten, twelve and thirteen). Ordination has meant the huge upheaval of three moves, so sadly, although their things are all here – they do not regard this town as their home, even if the house is. They still do need considerable support as young adulthood can be tough – financially, practically, emotionally. I do as much as I can to be there as needed. I miss them hugely, see them as often as possible, and adore each of them. That is not the point, but would people ask male clergy the same questions – in such a loaded way? Questions have been asked about my sexuality too, but more obliquely.

It's the deviousness of the church I find difficult. There's a painful, difficult mismatch between church and gospel. Churches can be old-fashioned but naturally inclusive. People can struggle with inclusion and be honest. That's so much better. None of them are bad people, it's the structures. Structures make you feel weird, awkward and inept. Personally, they make you feel a failure, and responsible. So much of what we are working with is fear.'

Michelle

'I would have preferred not to have a gender, but I lived in a society where binary gender is compulsory, so chose that which was not chosen for me. Eventually, I found the two models of gender difficult to understand, because people are not always clear-cut. I found it increasingly difficult to make the effort to give out the signals that denote female rather than male. These days I can be referred to as male by one person, and female the next. I don't correct people, because they are not wrong.

I have come around full circle through transition. I started out with some genital ambiguity, nowadays known as "XY-DSD", of uncertain aetiology, and my male assignment was reinforced surgically and socially. I went through adolescence as male, and spent part of my adult life living as a man: when I transitioned to female, it was to discover I was intersex all along, and I decided that intersex was a truer reflection of my identity.

The way we are, in our bodies, and the mind that is an integral part of them, is our being, our existence, our essence, and our spirit. This cannot be encapsulated in the dry categories of academia: this is the living flesh of which we are made. We become what others see in us. The role of medicine has been to categorise, define, dissect and describe us – to take us apart, reduced from the whole. Intersex has been defined as something alien and other, something to be studied, modified, corrected and conformed. This approach of defining terms and allocating categories, then applying them as if they in some way define who one is, strips people of their humanity; it is dehumanising, and rests on an a priori premise that intersex people are in some way intrinsically deficient, deformed and wrong.

The process of definition becomes a channel through which intersex people can be assessed, judged, manipulated, and coerced. Experts become assessors, seeing how well individuals correspond with their definitions, and put them through tests, in order to see how well they can fit within the categories deemed as acceptable (even to see if some can pass as "transsexual"). Intersex people have not been listened to, allowed to describe themselves, or consulted on what is best for them. This is because the expert is the "objective observer", while the "observed subject" has been regarded as inferior, not fit to judge what is in their own best interests. The evidence is clear – children have been assigned and treated in certain ways, without asking what they themselves might want. Adults have been given a limited range of options, and limited ways of pursuing them. Theory, and the evidence selected to justify theory, is asserted as being more significant than the experience of those subjected to the practical consequences of theory.

Intersex disturbs our notions about fixed, discrete, binary opposites in gender, just as much as transgendering the boundaries between male and female can. For those who have had some of these experiences, and who find it difficult to clearly identify as male or female, the need for a space in our society that is "other" than male or female is obvious. Sadly, it is the legacy of Church teaching that there are two inflexible sexes that cannot be changed or intertwined that has prevented society from achieving such a space in the way some traditional cultures have. Rather than embracing the "other", those outside the constraints of sex and gender, the Church still seems to want to pretend that those who are different do not exist. Denying that people exist erases their humanity.'[1]

*

In very different ways, Michelle and Billie blur categories and so are disturbing to others. They are both therefore subject to forms of policing, albeit of different kinds. Billie is expected to be more like a man in order to make the grade as a priest, but at the same time she is treated as a female sexual object as a single parent – apparently unattached, available, and with commitments to her children that cannot be easily understood. The sexual harassment she experiences seems to be a way of keeping her in her place, or to spring from a confusion about what her 'place' is. Michelle, as someone born with an indeterminate sex/gender, experiences being made to fit a singular category by physically violent means, in order for everyone else to feel comfortable with her.

Labels and Boxes

Anna

'I am an ordained trans woman. Throughout selection and training, I experienced very acutely the dynamic of "the other". Othering suggests danger and threat. There was an understanding within my sponsoring diocese that they would not let me be "hung out to dry". They guaranteed me a job. This may sound positive, but it suggested that I was *so* other that they went outside their own protocols. That's not what I wanted.

I am the kind of person who needs to feel special and different, but the other dynamic I experienced was that of being invested with magical properties. As a trans person you are totemic – occupying liminality in that gendered identity, and transcending gender. There is also much fetish-making that goes on. Desire shades into taboo. Trans people are *the* most fetishised sub-category amongst many. Male to female trans people are seen to be making of themselves their own sexual object. There is a small group of straight men who are obsessed with us, with websites dedicated to their pursuit of trans women.

I was required by the church to see a psychiatrist, specifically to do with being trans. Despite the fact that over a ten-year period before selection for ministry I had seen all the medical representatives of normality – somehow that didn't count. This all contributed to the "singled outness" that I felt during the ordination process. I hope trans people are not being medicalised in that way now, ten years on.

Through all this there is a lack of recognition for who we are. The institution has gifts and goods to dispense (i.e. jobs). It's powerful. I was asked to delay my ordination for a year, because of a shortage of stipendiary curacies. There were all sorts of reasons given about why this would be "good" for me. But I didn't see it that way. I experienced the institution as patronising and patriarchal, making decisions on my behalf. I experienced the same thing again after teaching on a spiritual directors' course in the Diocese. I taught a sexuality module. I told my personal story, exposing my vulnerability, as one human being to another, and they freaked. They perceived me to be offering my "exoticness" inappropriately, then went behind my back to report me to the 'higher ups' (the bishops) who then, in a very unprofessional way, asked me not to teach the course anymore, without ever discussing the issues openly and in an up-front way with me.'

Charlotte

The only way I can think to capture the complexity of my reality is through this poem:

Found Out

Single, heterosexual, engaged, married, divorced, single mum,
lesbian, civil partner, cis partner, queer…
Which label are you putting on me today?
This is my story, this is my truth
It is why I don't fit your assumptions and labels
It is why I am simply me.

Single young woman with a sexuality which is assumed.
Heterosexual the identity you sought to push upon me in the
church
Engaged the status when I accepted your model
Married the person who tried to do it your way.

Divorced the result of marrying too young,
When he went off with somebody else
And I could no longer pretend I was not a young gay woman.
Yet still I tried to play your game
Single mother repressing her sexual identity
Clinging to the idea that celibacy was what was required.

Then I fell in love,
A feeling of being who I truly was
Yet my partner was still repressing
That which was within them
Until one day the truth burst out…
The person I thought was a she
Was actually a he
Forced by society into conforming to the norms and values
Of wearing a body which didn't fit.

Confused legal understandings of gender where the birth
certificate was key
Passport designation ignored and a civil partnership ensued.
Then the law changed and the church whilst sympathetic
Didn't get the cis gay partner married to the trans guy.
Forced now to change my status to married

So he can go forward and get his gender recognition certificate
With the world and church seeing us as a straight couple.

Yet I am still a gay woman and he is a bisexual trans man.
We are a queer couple who don't fit into your boxes.
We are a couple who live beyond your simplistic definitions.
We are us – him and me – living it our own loving, monogamous way.

I think that the voices of the cis partners of trans people have been sadly missing in public discourse. Much of the research around trans issues has been done by trans and gender-queer researchers and this may be one reason for the apparent invisibility of cis partners. The experience of partners can invoke feelings of guilt but also disrupt the dominant discourse of the trans community. For many cis partners it appears that there are feelings of loss and grief involved. There can be a sense of confusion surrounding their own identity, and often feelings of loss of the loved one they knew. I identified as lesbian when I met my partner and the world initially saw us as a lesbian couple, but now the world sees us as a straight couple and I identify us as a queer couple. Partners may feel grief because, as with parents, they often see transition as a living death. This is one of the reasons for a reluctance to research the cis partner's experience. It is obviously particularly difficult for the trans community as they do not see transition in these terms and indeed some trans people can find the language expressed in relation to this insulting. But the feelings are real.'

*

Labels and boxes are double-edged. We embrace certain identity categories and feel liberated by them when they help us to express important things about who we are and where we belong. Especially when we are part of minority and oppressed groups. But these must be self-selected and self-defined. And they need to be elastic enough to incorporate the complexities of difference within the oppressed group. If such differences are eclipsed by the need to present a unified front, new forms of marginalisation emerge.

Further Reflections

How much can we be trusted to know ourselves, and who can be so trusted? This seems to be a key question for the Christian community. One of the things that used to frustrate me when I was in a lesbian relationship was the apparent contestability of my reality. 'Are you sure you're a lesbian?', 'How do you know?', 'You don't look or seem like a lesbian', 'Why do you think you're a lesbian?', 'What caused you to be a lesbian?' 'Are you sure you're not mistaken?'. If you are not normatively heterosexual, your testimony and self-understanding are not accepted at face value. Imagine a straight married man going through the process of selection for ordination. He declares himself to be happily married. No doubt there will be some testing of that in terms of exploration and questioning both of him and his spouse (whether you think that is appropriate or not is another matter). But the operative assumption would not be, 'Hmmm, this is rather dodgy. He declares himself to be happily married. I bet there's more to this than meets the eye.' Such an immediate hermeneutic of suspicion would not be deployed. Yet Sally, embracing by choice a life of singleness and celibacy, was met with a response of bewilderment and hyper-scrutiny by her Advisory Panel. And those who are in gay relationships have faced intrusive questioning from bishops and others about the most intimate aspects of their private sexual and relational lives to ensure *they really are aware* of the rules. There is a profound lack of trust at work, and a patronising sense that the institution knows best.

So Anna, a transgender woman who had gone through the long and gruelling process of jumping through all the medical and psychiatric hoops necessary to transition, was put through yet another hoop by a selection system that could have trusted her (not to mention trusting other professionals rather than needing a 'church approved' psychiatrist to be final arbiter). Who is likely to best understand Anna at that point in her life – herself, or a medic meeting her for the first time, or a bishop with little firsthand knowledge of gender variance? For intersex and transgender people in particular, the struggle to be believed has been a long and tortuous one. As Michelle powerfully describes, 'objective experts' have made decisions on behalf of intersex people, who have not been listened to, allowed to describe themselves or consulted about what is best for them. And Hannah, an autistic woman, encounters a form of therapy that is being imposed on those like her to prevent them being who they are and behaving in ways that are authentic to their createdness in God.

Anna's experience of being 'singled out' for special treatment during her selection and training process is part of a much bigger picture. If we are not really trusted to know and understand ourselves, then we won't be trusted to know what is 'best for us'. I have sat in many clergy deployment meetings where senior church leaders have made decisions on behalf of the clergy in their care about which jobs they should be given, and which placements would suit them. 'It wouldn't be fair to send her there. She's not really resilient enough to deal with the dynamics in that parish. They haven't really got their heads around women's ministry yet'; 'I am not sure this is the best place for him. I don't think that village is ready for a Black priest.'; 'That community will really punish a priest in a civil partnership. They clearly need a married man with children.' These decisions may be well intentioned, but what is lacking is input from the person whose future is being determined by the conversation. They are likely to have given much deeper thought to the issues being raised than the senior leaders, because it is *their* lived reality and *their* future.

If your declared sense of yourself is neither believed nor trusted – if, in effect, your integrity is called into question – it is hard to feel accepted or acceptable. As women (and marginalised men), we live with a sense that our very being is contested. In Chapter Two we explored Mary Hunt's suggestion that sexual violence is contextual, not episodic, and that we will not be able to combat abuse until we understand that. So we need to understand that a deep sense of not being *good enough* is the context in which women and LGBTI+ people live out their faith. Amanda cited an episode – an occasion when visiting the USA – when she tasted what it felt like to be free of the sense of not being good enough. She drew an analogy between contextual oppression and chronic pain. It becomes so much a part of your life that you don't realise it's there until it lifts for a short while, and gives you a sense of how amazing life could be if you were to finally experience full inclusion.

The other obvious outworking of not feeling 'good enough' is that you feel the need to hide. You are silenced. There are complex layers of silencing described in the stories. If, against the backdrop of your sexuality not being good enough (which I would argue holds true for all women), you also experience abuse, then the potential burden of shame is huge. How to believe that God loves you when your visceral reality is that you are unlovable? And how then to avoid a silencing of God within, a silencing between you and God in prayer, and a silencing of yourself within community? And if you are a lesbian priest charged with keeping the confidences of those whose 'cure of souls' is your responsibility, yet are expected also to hide your very self and your relational life in the process, how can this be a sustainable way of life?

Yet there is a conviction within these stories that God's love and acceptance is distinct from that of the church. Whilst the latter may remain elusive, the former (as we shall see in the next chapter) can still be vibrant and real. Women's faith journeys and spiritual growth can happen within the church, but also away from church. This does not detract, though, from the need for church to become more outward-facing, inclusive, caring, engaged, real and honest.

Chapter Four

Reclaiming Spirit

Reflection

Human touch is fraught with confusion, risk of misunderstanding and the potential for exploitation. Yet you chose touch to bring healing. Sometimes you healed by touching, and other times you healed by not needing to. You knew which was appropriate and when. You also knew when someone had touched you.

God's love and power flowed through you, and touch was the conduit, the channel, the focus. God touched people through his connection with you, and made them whole and clean and free when the world considered them worthless. The world told the woman with the flow of blood and the leper that they were unclean. Their fate was public denigration. They lived in the shadows, avoiding attention. You brought them into the open, so everyone knew that they were restored. It was official, it was public. The woman knew that to touch your cloak would be enough – that it would bring her close enough to the grace and power that she could see conducted through you. The leper knelt before you and invited you to choose to heal him. You did so choose, and you stretched out your hand to him, made physical contact with one whom others considered to be contaminated.

Touch was also your way of 'speaking' with those who could not communicate through conventional means. For the deaf man who could not talk, you put your fingers into his ears. You were giving him a sign of what you planned to do for him. And you spit and touched his tongue, a symbol that you were giving him the power to speak. And with the man born blind, you made mud on the ground with dust and your saliva, and touched his eyes with it. He would have felt the viscous grit and known that transformation was coming.

All these were glimpses of intimate, embodied, human connections through which God worked. And often that work went against the grain of social convention and expectation. You brought a touch of subversion to the human values that surrounded you.

Negotiating our Heritage

Lilith

'I think I've ended up with a God who is completely beyond gender, sexuality or any other of the things we use to put down other people – unknowable but close if that makes sense.

I have been driven back to the local, encultured, lived religion of my childhood (village Church of England) which had so little to do with clergy, and a lot to do with place and real lives. Except so few churches achieve that now. So where is there to go? I long for local churches to be returned to the people who care about them, and used by them to engage with what is sacred to them, in a plurality of ways, whilst respecting the tradition of the place.

As for the God question, I don't think a transcendent God is any less real or accessible, and I think I find God far more distant and unknowable the longer I live. The very opposite of the "what a friend we have in Jesus" kind of God who seems like a busy neighbour and all-too-human but grander. God is "not this, not that" as the Hindus say.'

Vivienne

'As I've got older, I've found it harder to pray. Everything in my head is so loud. I still try, but I don't know who I'm talking to.

I never thought I'd marry a Christian, because I never met a Christian man who I'd like to spend my life with. It's all so lazy and complacent, Christian language. People who aren't Christians just let it all flow out, somehow. That's much more attractive to me.

The man I married is a Muslim. Meeting him was so interesting, because it's as though he calls me back towards God in a way nobody else has. He really works at it. There is something about Islam that means you are continually trying to connect with God.

Because he doesn't believe in sex before marriage, it made me question myself. Have I been a slut, throwing myself about? I tried to do no sex before marriage, but realised I was doing it for him, not for me. I don't believe there is one rule that's right for everybody. We're all so different.

My faith has changed since being with him. He interrogates my faith, and has made me realise I don't really know what I believe. He wanted to know whether I thought that Jesus is God's son? Do I? I realise that my ancestors were colonised and gave us Christianity. If not for that, what would I believe now? I'd believe in a God of sun, of rain, of harvest, probably. We cannot know.'

Kezia

'I worked a long time with older women in my church who told me many stories about how they were oppressed by the mainstream ideas of the church. And I talk a lot about this subject with my best friend, also a pastoral worker, now aged eighty-five. When I started reading the Bible I was amazed to find almost nothing negative about sexuality. What do all the Christians base their negative ideas on? I really don't know. My friend and I think that the big problem is making God separate from yourself, and against you. It is difficult to find new words for God. Or maybe the words are not so new, but we don't have the power or the places to speak in another way about God.'

Rebecca

'Every Sunday I go to church is a struggle. We have a Wednesday evening Eucharist followed by a meal for a small group of people who live on the margins and often counter to church [or Christian] convention. If I hadn't had exposure to feminist theology, without those safe spaces, I would have had to leave the church or retrench. So for me the "should I stay or should I go" question is very real. I still live with that question.

Five Rhythms dancing is my core, embodied spiritual practice. We need a meta-narrative that holds us when we reject what the church offers us. Society is losing all those structures and rhythms that faith offered in the past. What will happen a couple of generations from now when people don't have any stories of faith to start with? What will people find to hold them? The church has been very bad at translating concepts and addressing the question of how to equip the laity.

My transgender partner and I would like to make our vows to each other as the people we are now. We have wondered about doing that in the church we attend. We could have pushed the church on that, tried to force the issue. But we don't want to use their words. We are rejecting what the church offers at these important times of our lives because what they offer does not fit our narrative, or reflect how we want to be thought of or named. If it's not doing that for us, then it's probably not doing it for most other people either. Our consumer capitalist society has let people down, people are desperate for some hooks to articulate the pain and the mess and the joy of life. Where is the church in all that? By not being there, it is letting people down too.'

Julianne

'I was raised in an atheist background, where faith was not merely disregarded but positively discouraged and ridiculed. My parents were both old-school Socialists who saw religion as a worse than useless force in the world, and very much aspired to raise my sister and I in the same vein. I was secretly dissatisfied with the stark limitations of this outlook by the time I reached my mid-teens – also the same time I became conscious that my depression was hugely if not entirely due to gender dysphoria – but I was too afraid of disappointing my family to come out either as an unfulfilled theist or as an unfulfilled trans woman.

I had enjoyed Romanticism studies during my undergraduate years, so chose to focus on P. B. Shelley for my doctorate. I encountered the idea that Shelley's works often express a longing for androgyny or the feminine and a frustration and (self) disgust with traditional masculine values. The theory that this was indicative either of a gender-fluid sense of identity or even an "imaginative transsexualism" had great personal resonance for me. I read of the influence of the figure of Christ on the imagination of the mature Shelley. He never saw Christ simply as a father figure to be toppled or even as a threatening masculine presence, but responded to a rich theological tradition of seeing Jesus as a feminine figure.

Encountering such passages was perhaps the first time I had a sense of faith – and of Jesus in particular – as reaching out to me, and affirming me in a way I had never known. My family's awareness of my gender identity – which I had been unable to perfectly conceal from them – had been expressed only in a mixture of embarrassed silence and in one case outright disgust. Both reactions had left me with the sense that my gender dysphoria was a shameful flaw to be fought or buried. These passages, by contrast, left me with a sense of acceptance, and proved a major step in guiding me towards Christianity.

In the course of attending various churches over several years, I would have to admit having met contrary opinions that very much emphasised the view of Jesus as an alpha-male exemplar, and of that template being appropriate to his male-born followers (and none other). Mercifully, I never found this view reconcilable with the biblical Jesus, who forbade his followers from committing violence even in his defence (and healed the consequences of such violence), educated and empowered his female followers, refused power and status himself, and paved the way for very "unmanly" men (such as the eunuch of Acts 8) to join the faith. I am now confirmed in the Anglican church, and finally attending services as myself (having been "out" for a year), in the course of which I have had this latter view strengthened, and have been warmly accepted by both clergy and laity. I have even, of late, encountered a trans ordinand within the local seminary (very inspiring, as I had given up hope I could ever be an acceptable candidate for ministry), and will be working with him to draft an affirmation ceremony for both of us – seemingly the first of its kind in the Church of Wales (though not unprecedented in the Anglican communion).'

Ruth

'As LGBT people we cannot rely on the Bible and tradition to tell us what we must think and feel about God, but need to look to our own experience and ask "what does my own experience teach me about God?" We must trust our own journey and be willing to share it with others. We have a gift to the Church and to the world, for apart from anything we are called to become missionaries to a homophobic world. When the psychoanalyst Carl Gustav Jung was asked whether he believed in God he replied: "*I don't believe, I know.*" Likewise, I speak from my own knowledge, my embodied knowledge.

I was brought up in a Catholic household. I remember at the age of seven or eight asking the priest why Jesus had been male rather than female. At the age of ten I went to boarding school, a convent, which had a very positive influence on me. The nuns were strong, intelligent, committed women who were not dependent on men for money or self-worth. I studied French and Spanish at university and in my third year I was able to spend a year abroad and I went to Chile, Latin America and worked with the Sisters of Mother Teresa.

I felt a strong pull towards Religious Life and in my early twenties I visited different Religious Orders to see which one I might join. At that time in my life, even though I had had a few boyfriends, I thought of myself more as asexual.

I decided to experience living in a community for a year – it was a lay community that was committed to working for social justice and living simply. It was during this year that I fell in love with a fellow community member, a woman, and she with me. It was very traumatic. I felt my whole world falling apart. So much of my identity had been built around being a good Catholic girl and suddenly I wasn't any more. I had an image of myself being on pillars which placed me up near God. At that point the pillars came crashing down and I found myself on the rubble.

About a year after I fell in love I went away on retreat. I wanted to know whether God loved me specifically as a lesbian. I needed to know that God loved me not just as a good Catholic woman. The answer came back in the form of two songs which I wrote, though I felt that it was actually the Holy Spirit working through me. One of the songs was about being made in the image of God. The other song had as its chorus these words:

> Do you not know that I love you,
> more passionately than any lover,
> And do you not know that my spirit is in you
> Just like it is in any other?

In order to accept that God loved me, however, I had to change my old image of God. Up to then I had an image of God which had been handed down to me, both consciously and unconsciously. God was male, white and heterosexual. There was no way that this God was going to approve of me loving another woman – at most this God would put up with it, but He would not rejoice with me. Since my most intimate relationships were with women, I felt that God, who I know is beyond gender and sexual orientation, nevertheless was in some way lesbian since I had been made in her image. Here was God then – my lover, a woman and one who would whoop with delight if I fell in love, someone I could be intimate with.'

*

Images of God are powerful, and give us a sense of who we are, and who we can become. Most of us hold an internal dialogue between our inherited ideas about God, and the God we experience to be real. Julianne felt the 'stark limitations' of an insistence that there is no God. Kezia spoke of not having the power or the places to speak in another way about God. Restrictions on what is allowed to be said and thought are key. Rebecca is clear about the limitations of the cathedral liturgy. She feels strongly that this would not be a place that could embrace or express her lived reality as the partner of a transgender woman. She could not be named, recognised, or her love and commitment spoken of through it. Ruth experienced the trauma of discovering herself to be lesbian whilst still having a sense that God was narrowly male, White and heterosexual. She needed to see something of herself in God to fully experience the unconditional love that God has for her. For Lilith, the journey has been away from a domesticated God, like human beings only bigger and better, towards something much less immediately knowable, though the possibility of closeness with this God remains. There is a certain freedom in God's transcendence – in not being able to pin God down, or make God too human, with all the finitudes that involves. It allows for uncertainty and not knowing; for a sense of mystery and a journey of discovery. God may be perceived as distant or as close, but the key commonality is in finding ways to connect, challenging inherited images of whatever kind, and finding ways to pray that are real for us. There is also a realisation that there is much in the Christian tradition that is friendly; that it has treasures within it, but these have often been hidden from us. For Ruth it was the strong female role models in her convent school. For Kezia it was the discovery that in reading the Bible for herself, she did not find the restrictions she had been led to believe were there. And Julianne discovered a feminine aspect to Jesus which enabled her to accept her own ambivalence about masculinity, and ultimately to feel a divine acceptance of her trans identity.

Inhabiting our Traditions

Deborah

I came to faith in a pretty standard evangelical Christian Union context. But that way of seeing things – the certainty, the sense that God dwells within pretty strict confines, the sense that we're entitled to determine who is and isn't saved, according to pretty clear criteria – stopped working for me really quite quickly. The most difficult transition in my life has not been coming out as gay, but coming out of a particular kind of evangelical certainty and being challenged to construct for myself something more flexible, creative, mysterious, risky, authentic and true.

I fell in love with the Church of England in a council estate parish. The liturgy was the folk song of the people – pared down, but authentic and powerful, reflecting the rhythm of the seasons and the liturgical year of which I knew nothing – a new world of colour and language and symbolism.

Father, of course, knew best. But his pronouncements were so manifestly preposterous that I rarely gave them headspace – clearly he was quite wrong, and that was the end of the matter. Against the backdrop of the arguments for women's equality – which have somehow been reduced to a much simpler argument about women's ministry – the antidote to his sermons was reading. Pointed in the right direction by kind Jesuits with whom I'd made friends during a year after university, working in a homelessness project in Whitechapel – I never really looked back.

I sometimes think the Church of England website, with its images of joyful, fulfilled, diverse Anglicans going about their business, should have a little disclaimer on the bottom, like Mr Kipling cake packets and estate agents' plans for new housing developments –

you know the kind of thing – "artist's impression", or "posed by models" or "serving suggestion". Because – honestly, it's a very long time since it's squared up with my reality.

So much of my own journey has been about trying to draw together an integrated and meaningful way. Over the years I've come to recognise that this search is one in which almost everyone is engaged. The way of faith which suggests that it's all about a pre-packaged bundle, which human experience has to fit into, where beliefs are static and certain and unchanging – that no longer works for me. It seems to me now that faith is not so much about hiding inside the ark and waiting to be rescued, as building a raft from whatever is serviceable and keeps you afloat, lashing on new pieces as they come your way, jettisoning the things that aren't of use any longer, even as you acknowledge that they've helped you on your journey so far. It's a more precarious way, but it's also more exhilarating, more real. You feel the wind on your face and hear the sounds of the water and experience life all around you. It's real. And you have to learn to keep your balance, and hold your nerve. But it's real. It's this idea of a constantly changing, dynamic system which needs to be maintained and nurtured and valued and treated with absolute respect and tenderness, which somehow takes things to another level for me.'

Naomi

'Seeing myself as a woman before God has been a constant thing for me. What's really hard is the current deconstruction of so many things – the Anglican church, the liturgy. This has happened around me. So much is happening so quickly. My language is lagging behind. In the midst of this deconstruction, some language holds, some language is quite hard. If, like me, you have to struggle hard for a sense of self, this deconstruction can be difficult.

All the churches are running at a different pace. I like structures – what's familiar. If every week I am offered something different, and every week I am already feeling bewildered, I don't know what to do with that. Even if I disagree with what's familiar, within structures I can feel present. Otherwise I feel invisible, to myself, to others, and to God.

I have become a Roman Catholic and have arrived home. Despite being counter-feminist, counter-intuitive, counter cultural, I have found a space where I don't have to apologise for being. For so many years I had to hide from God, feeling more and more estranged. I had been suicidal and sectioned because of the sexual violation I experienced. There is a painting by Sieger Köder of Mary Magdalene, hiding behind a rock. I saw myself in that picture because I couldn't say anything or tell anybody, and therefore that bit of me didn't exist. I felt shame and humiliation, especially about having a body that responds. The survivor community helped. But it is hard work being a survivor.

It's hard to tell about one's abuse, because it's a very private thing, not something I'd readily share. It's as intimate as being with my husband, though for different reasons, and I wouldn't speak about that either. When I thought I was dying (after receiving a diagnosis of cancer) I didn't want that to happen without sorting out what I could. It was very hard to be in church, especially in my city, so I stepped away from it. Studying for a Masters was my salvation. It gave me a voice, a way to express what my silences were. With people of all ages and different cultures.

When I was an Anglican, it got to the stage when it was so painful to be around church. Everyone knew me and everyone knew my abuser. I couldn't be myself. At every turn I couldn't be me. I stopped going anywhere, being with people. The church I got married in, and used to go to, is the one where my abuser now worships.

It was through social networking that I found a Catholic religious that I could have good 'God conversations' with. I began reading scripture again and praying again. Properly – not the arid prayers I prayed before. I don't feel compromised as a feminist because it's given me my life back. I can go there and be me, and be me in front of God. The catechism reshaped my warped and distorted thinking. The catechism demystified God for me.

Making my first confession, I was able to say, "I can't forgive her", and I walked out feeling that I'd put a bag down. I'd listened to myths about what the Roman Catholic Church says. But I found that I could be with God in all my neediness and brokenness. My first confession was utterly profound.

The person who took me through the Catholic catechism, a Dominican, is an academic. I needed the intellect, because if things get too sore, you can step back into that. He listened, he taught me, and spoke into some of my experience. There is an integrity in stepping away from something destructive, and there was a freedom for me in becoming Catholic.

Somebody's cracked something open for me. I'm going somewhere, and I'm not hiding behind that rock anymore. It has even had an impact on my relationship with my husband, because I've got freed from something. I find in the Roman Catholic Church that you're not condemned for what you can't do.

I find that where I go now for Mass is familiar. I know what the order of service is. I know exactly what's going to happen and when. I've been to churches where unexpected things happen, and I get trapped in a space in rows. Having river banks is good for me, not being on a flood plain at risk of being swept away.'

Esther

'Evensong and compline are my favourite offices. It is important to keep them, but with the person-power being limited, covering eight churches as my team does, we need to look at different kinds of leadership and authority. We have a twenty-four hour society, and it's very difficult to sustain the pattern of life and worship that we've historically offered. What else can we do to enable people to make sense of their faith?

Debate with those of no faith and of different faiths really stimulates me. God is indefinable, so no one view of God is right.

I am an oblate in the Order of Julian of Norwich (OJN). It's based on contemplative prayer. I like a rule of life because within those boundaries I feel free. The vows I have taken are of poverty, chastity, obedience and prayer. It's one of the few orders that doesn't take a stand on same sex couples, sex and sexuality. They try to model the way that Julian sees God.

New monastic communities are increasing in popularity. There is a need for being part of a community, including those that are not geographically based. Faith can be found in church, but many people leave. But the more people say, "this is what I want and need from you", the more likely the church is to change. Unless we know what people are expecting, we won't change. I can see why people leave church. If it wasn't for my calling, I'm not sure I'd be part of it. Sometimes it's hard to stay within the rules. We are there to hold and represent something bigger. We need to be more flexible, speaking of God. I see my role as finding ways to speak God into people's lives, in whatever way they can hear it. Evangelism can be pushy, and used to have a language all of its own. But that's changing now and we can learn from that. When I was a nurse, I learned to treat people with love and respect. That's what the church needs to do – and what it often tries to do.'

Amber

'Whilst I was studying to be a social worker, we had some lectures about sexuality and gender studies, as separate and distinct, and talked about the social construction of gender. It was as if suddenly things became clear in my mind that I was not gay (that is, a gay man trying to be heterosexual), but was actually transgender, and that the issues that I had been struggling with were due to being trans. I discussed this with my partner, and later told her that I wanted to change gender.

I started going to a Metropolitan Community Church, as well as my Catholic Church, and met other trans people there. My partner and I went to a lecture about the Gender Recognition Act, which had recently come into force. I went to talk to my GP about getting a referral to a gender clinic, then saw a gender specialist who diagnosed me as having gender dysphoria. It was as if the pieces of my life were falling into place. For a while I stopped going to the Catholic Church as I did not want to be transitioning and experiencing the guilt that I felt the Catholic Church would lay on me.

I started working as a social worker in my new gender and having changed my name, and I had gender reassignment surgery three years later. I have battled at times with various mental health crises, and had a further psychotic episode just after my fortieth birthday. There was a watershed moment for my partner and I at that time, as she realised that she had carried for ten years the thought that I did not want to be with her. The emotion of this release was too much for me emotionally.

My faith has changed somewhat over the last year, and I now also go to a Buddhist Centre, as well as going to the Catholic Church, and when I can I go to the Cathedral. I struggle to believe in an all powerful "God", but believe that everyone on this planet is part of the Divine Spirit, whether they live true to that or not. Much of my reluctance to name "God" I believe comes from the early engagement with my parents not having God's love in their relationship. In the Catholic Church I am aware that I stand very much on the margins, but refuse to let this go because I believe that people have to be in organisations if they want to see change. I stay mainly because I have a strong devotion to Mary as Theotokos, the mother of the Divine Spirit within each of us.'

*

Naomi and Esther both find freedom in a rule of life. For Naomi it is an antidote to the change and linguistic evolution that is happening across denominations, the unpredictability and the risk that comes with spontaneity. For Esther it is the structure and discipline in which freedom is found. A Christian tradition that Amber found inimical in her time of gender transition is, for Naomi, the key to her healing. She has had something life-giving 'cracked open' for her that enables her to emerge from her hiding place behind a rock, set her burden down and live again. It has enabled her to make peace with the theological conundrum which is Christian approaches to forgiveness – she no longer feels condemned for what she cannot do. For her, it involves certain things to remain the same – reliable, unchanging. As she says, as one who struggles for a sense of self, deconstruction of faith and language can be difficult and bewildering. For her it is preferable to live within structures – the river banks that save her from the flood plain, where things are chaotic and uncontrolled, even if she doesn't always assent to the structures or agree with them. For her, the catechism has demystified God.

Other women, such as Deborah, need the opposite approach. She embraces pragmatism and constant change; the creativity of improvising as you go along, sitting light to tradition. Faith is like a raft, keeping one afloat in a stream of constant change. She seeks an integrated and meaningful way. Ultimately, both approaches are about finding the trusted ground from which to undertake a spiritual journey – the place of relative safety from which we can feel secure enough to explore. For some of us safety comes through structures, for others it comes through being able to cast formerly oppressive structures aside.

Loving Ourselves

Deborah

There have been many times when I have lost sight of myself as a child of God, reflecting God's image, created for glory, and for fullness of life; fearfully and wonderfully made, a part of the body of Christ, the dwelling place of the Almighty, already loved by God before I was put together in my mother's womb. There have been times when I have decided it would be a good idea to ignore all that, and instead work my way to salvation; times when I have decided that the smart choice would be to deny myself, take up my cross, and work myself ragged, because somehow that was the way of holiness.

What if we were to reflect on what it might mean for each of us to know what knocks us off balance? And what is it about the combination of women and church which can so easily lead to us neglecting ourselves, losing sight of ourselves? It seems to me that there's a strong tradition of Christian asceticism which casts a long shadow over all of us, and perhaps especially – or maybe distinctively – women. It's hard to know which came first – the message of patriarchy reminding you that you're not quite up to the job, the Christian tradition which emphasises sin over grace, or just the daily experience of living as a woman in an ever more complex world. I'm not sure. I know none of this will come as breaking news; in a way we are all living out this complex and dangerous dynamic. And that is why it bears repeating: love yourself. Your very self.

This fragile ecology of our hearts and minds has so many parts, and valuing and attending to all of them, simultaneously, is a tall order. Keeping in balance our need for sleep, nourishment, stimulation, nurture, touch, acceptance, affirmation, a sense of meaning, opportunities for reflection, for transcendence, for colour, for fresh air, for companionship...balanced with the 'givens' of our health, ability to support ourselves financially, support those who depend on us, maintain a living space, exist across a range of different locations and contexts, make sense of different networks of people, adapting and relating to each of them in constantly changing ways, learning and developing new skills, balancing the promises and demands of competing political and faith systems, making a choice amongst many choices, living with choices we wouldn't have chosen ourselves, coming to terms with our own limitations, and our own littleness in the face of things, and with the little person inside. This is a complex system. But this is how we have been created, and we were created for glory, and for goodness and for fullness of life. And all of this is utterly, utterly known by God. So there must be a way of holding it all together.

I have recently experimented with reflexology, having been rather cynical of such complementary therapies. It has been gentle and powerful all at once, and I am intrigued and fascinated and curious about what it will tell me, about what my body has to tell me that I've learned to ignore. My body seems eager to talk, and I'm ready to listen, at last.

During my first session, I had a real sense of sadness that the Christian faith has lost touch with the wisdom of the body. That the chart on the wall had Buddhist symbols, because as Christians we've somehow walked away from this wisdom, this way of knowing God. This seemed to me both a corporate sadness, and a personal one – that my faith community has so far prevented me from engaging with something which might just help, might be a source of healing and wholeness for me, and for others. I don't think I'm ready to embrace the crystals just yet, but it's the start of a journey, a re-evaluation of sorts, a discovery, a confession, and an invitation to begin to value the other, the complementary, the different paths, in ways I've failed to do before.'

Lydia

'I have been going to church for about six years, but I don't feel as though I have a concept of God that fits church. I like the liturgy, but I don't really talk to people at church because I feel like you have to behave a certain way, and if I speak I might be thrown out.

I suffered a lot of sexual abuse as a child, and I used to say the Lord's prayer back then, and I did believe in God, but I ended up back in church through a love affair. The force of what I have come to call 'Godly love' was so strong and powerful I was completely taken over by it, and it's then that I became convinced that God is love.

I was broken hearted through that relationship, and was searching for a way forward. I began the discernment process for the priesthood, but I was told that I was so far out and off-centre that I would never get anywhere with it. I'm the kind of person who needs to try things out for their truths. If I haven't gone and turned over that stone over there, how can I trust it? The church didn't want that approach to faith.

As soon as I felt that love bursting through, I was already praying, but in a very bodily kind of way. That love is found in the erotic, the life-force, vitality – that's all deeply central for me. If you don't integrate your lustful and angry parts, you're cutting yourself off at the roots, and abuse proliferates. There's nothing about me that God can't cope with, and that force is essentially good.'

*

It is easy to say that we have been created for fullness of life, that God loves everything about us. But how do we connect with it, day to day, living as we do in a world that suggests we are not good enough? For if we were good enough, we wouldn't need anything or desire anything more, and our economies demand infinite desire, restless dissatisfaction. To have enough and to be enough, and to be convinced of it, is hard.

Deborah lays out for us a methodology by which we can begin to understand for ourselves what disrupts our own 'fragile ecology of heart and mind'. This is an important and potentially subversive spiritual practice. It enables us to connect with those aspects of our faith tradition which convince, and reconvince us of our infinite belovedness in God, our preciousness, our uniqueness, our sense of being fearfully and wonderfully made, intentionally created for a purpose, with a calling and a set of gifts which nobody else has; the very things that are under attack from the contextual denigration and devaluation that assails us. Lydia wants a faith that can be trusted, and it can only be trusted if all aspects have been tested – all the stones turned over. She finds this approach is not welcomed by religious power structures that demand that we put our trust in external authorities. But Godly love and prayer were returned to her through the experience of broken heartedness. She believes in a God that values the erotic as the vital life force; in the integration of lust and anger to combat abuse, and she has a sure faith that nothing is outwith God, and there is nothing within her that God does not love.

Being Human, Being Real

Jenny

A hospice chaplain tells the story of Jenny:

'A year before I met her, Jenny had been working as an air hostess. Although she had been in this work for many years, she never got tired of donning her smart uniform, putting on her make-up and high-heels and doing her hair in a stylish "up-do", in order that she looked as glamorous and well-turned-out as possible.

Suddenly, her world was turned upside-down by the diagnosis of a cancerous brain tumour. Although she had had to stop working, over the two years since her diagnosis the company were very good to her, allowing her to take free flights to any destination of her choice while she was still well enough to travel.

She underwent various forms of treatment in the hope of a cure but, sadly, this was not to be; and she had had to face the reality that her condition was terminal, with all the physical, psychological and spiritual implications which this brought with it.

Fortunately, she became a service-user at a Sue Ryder hospice where she attended the weekly "day hospice" sessions, and occasionally came onto the ward as an in-patient. Here she found the support she needed, and she eventually died peacefully at home, as was her wish.

I was the chaplain when Jenny first started to come to Day Hospice. I remember my first meeting with her vividly. A softly-spoken, friendly lady, she was coming to terms with the fact that she could no longer walk, and had to use a wheelchair. Added to this, the drug-therapy she had been receiving had caused her weight to increase hugely, and she had lost all her hair. Her carer had got her dressed in a bit of a hurry that morning and her wig was crooked. She asked me if I would straighten it for her, which I did.

As she told me her story, I couldn't help but be struck by the enormous changes which had taken place in her life. She described her pre-diagnosis identity as having been that of a healthy, active, glamorous, professional, independent lady. Her post-diagnosis self was, she said, a different person altogether. Now she could no longer work, and had to depend on others for her daily needs, she was wrestling with the question, "Who am I?"

It was clear that Jenny's self-esteem was at rock bottom. She no longer felt she was of any value, because so much of her previous identity had been bound up with her work, and with her appearance. Although she had a deep faith, and said she was not afraid of dying, it occurred to me that it was the problem of how to live – how to find meaning, value and purpose in her life as it was now – which was distressing her the most.

It was as though the landscape of her life had been irrevocably changed, from one where she thought she knew the route she was taking, and was journeying accordingly, to one where that landscape had become hostile and unfamiliar. There were no landmarks any more, and she felt lost and unable to see the way forward.

As I talked with Jenny, I happened to notice her fingernails. They were beautifully shaped, but the nail-varnish was chipped. I asked her whether anyone did her nails for her regularly. She replied that, no, although she had a friend who had done them for her a couple of months before, that friend lived many miles away and she didn't think she'd be seeing her for a long time. She joked that, "At least now I don't do any housework, my manicure lasts longer!"

I said to her, "Well, I'm not a professional manicurist, but I've had a few manicures in my time. Would you like me to do your nails for you next week?" The joy on her face, which absolutely lit up at my suggestion, almost brought me to tears. That such a simple thing could mean so much…and yet, of course, it wasn't just a simple thing. I realised that, in some way, this was about reclaiming her sense of identity and dignity.'

Rachel

'The truth I discovered through SRS (Sex Reassignment Surgery) is that surgery doesn't change sex, it confirms it. For all practical purposes I'd already become a woman. In my head I was already a woman. As far as my family were concerned I was already a woman. The surgery genuinely mattered because it allowed me to begin to relax. It took away a huge fear of exposure. And, most of all, it enabled me to begin to enjoy my body properly. Like almost every woman in Western culture, there were and are things about my body I dislike…For good or ill, that is commonly how it is to be a woman in our society – whether trans or not. But for the first time ever as a woman I could live with some bodily confidence. I was not ashamed of what lay between my legs. I was a body and it was truly good…Give me bodies – wobbling, wrinkly, stretch-marked, even surgically enhanced bodies. Bodies enjoying themselves. Bodies unfrightened of their possibilities. God has no fear of bodies. This is the truth at the heart of the incarnated God. The idea of God emptying him- or herself into fragile flesh is one of the great shocks of Christian theology.'[1]

Michelle

'I have come to see walking a middle way between the sexes as my path. It is a path between two compulsory genders, another way, a narrow way, a difficult place, but the only place I can genuinely be. It is like living in a crack in the world from which comes a specific type of knowledge and power. But, as a realisation, it is not about what I have become, but the way I am, the way I always was. It is how it has always been for me, physically, mentally, and emotionally, and reflects things about me from when I was born, before somebody decided to correct the ambiguities in me. Finding and being myself is like a religious calling, because this is how it was meant to be. This middle way between genders should sit comfortably within any spiritual path or discipline, drawing strength from both genders instead of just one, not as a third, but as a path between genders, knowing gender is illusory, socially constructed.'[2]

Anna

'As for life on the ground, in the parish: most people want to be loved, and they want to love their priest. They want their priest to be vulnerable. To be human. Being a gay woman is seen as positive. It's human. There are people who wish I talked about sex and gender less, but also see that this comes out of being authentically me, and that means they can be authentically them.

As a queer woman within this institution, I am claiming my own power, claiming my own voice. People will make up all sorts of shit about me. None of us can control those narratives. My biggest fear was that nobody would stand next to me. Coming out as who I am is liberation for ministry, for who God is. Offering, in a leadership sense, a narrative that others can inhabit. My giftedness is found also in the other dimension of my life as a poet. My queerness in the secular poetry world, talking about gender and sexuality is possible as a confident, public intellectual, with no apology. In that world, it's being religious that is treated as unusual. The connective tissue between the institution of the church and the arts and culture has gone. The institution is too lacking in sophistication. It is flat and obsessed with its own survival.'

*

Deborah talked of her sadness that the Christian faith has lost touch with the wisdom of the body, and this way of knowing God. And Jenny's story shows us that something as apparently 'trivial' as the state of one's finger nails, can be symbolic of the whole process by which we know and value ourselves, inhabit a sense of identity, and affirm who we are. Our bodily selves are fragile, constantly changing, mortal. Everything is temporary. We undergo massive transitions. How can our spirituality enable us to embrace this reality – the pathos of the cycle of life in which we are all caught up, in which death and disintegration bring new life?

Our inherited faith has de-emphasised embodiment, and not enabled us to fully inhabit ourselves. In redressing this imbalance, however, there is no hint here that we need to de-emphasise the intellect – the need to love God with all our minds. Rather, the stories in this chapter manifest the integration of feelings and the intellect. Julianne discovered a femininity in Jesus that was crucial in her faith journey through studying the poet Shelley. Naomi needed an academic approach to the catechism as a place to step back into if her feeling world got too sore as she explored her faith. Amber came to an understanding of herself as transgender through social work studies, particularly the concept of gender as a social construction. Deborah's antidote to restrictive ideas encountered through her male priest was reading, initially books recommended by a Jesuit friend. And Anna finds a bigger, freer world in which to be herself as a priest through being a public intellectual and a poet. But this work is always held in balance with embodiment. Many experience faith as demanding a disembodied approach to life, and this is challenged here by, for instance, an encounter with reflexology, by five rhythms dancing, and by various forms of artistic creativity such as poetry and songwriting. Anna's diagnosis of the church, that it is 'flat and obsessed with its own survival' has the corollary that the connective tissue between it and the arts has been lost. You cannot be a disembodied artist, for creativity demands that you are open to your whole self, channelling that self into your work. Reclaiming spirit means embracing a faith that is integrated, holistic, artistic and embodied.

Chapter Five

Recreating Faith

Reflection

Our Father Who Art in Heaven?
OUR father...
Full beam ahead,
The floodlights shine
On the perimeter fence of faith.
Self-appointed police are on patrol,
Thinking that their meticulous surveillance
Is necessary
To protect God
From the incursions
of heresy and slander,
And the suggestion that God is a lie.
'God is ours', they say,
'We can describe him to you.
We know all about Him.
You can know God through us.'

God says, 'You are mine. All of you.
I chose you.
But do not cling to me
As a weapon, or a possession, or a toy.
Do not use your allegiance to me
to separate you from others.

Found Out

*You do not know who else I choose,
or why,
or for what purpose.
I belong to everybody, and to nobody.
Release me to be a mystery
And then you will know me.'*

Our FATHER...
How many words does it take
To change a lifetime
Of thinking
That there's just one word for everything
And that my word
Is the right word
And the only word?

'It is finished'
Three words to open up
a whole new vocabulary...
A is for Abba – father,
But the new alphabet does not end there.

God says, 'call me what you wish
For I know where your words come from.
I know their derivation, and their destination.
Call me mother, lover, friend
Call me sanctity and grace
Call me love, justice, mercy
Your words will never fill the space
That is me.

Who ART in heaven...
The statue of liberty is.
She stands,
A static symbol
of freedom.

She reaches for the sky,
But has feet of stone.
She stands firm against the elements –
The ocean's waves, the wind, the rain and the sun.
Reminders that nothing stays still.

To be or not to be
Is not really the question.
The question is,
What difference does it make, to be?
What difference does it make that we are?
What difference does it make,
When God lives
Not as a marble statue, frozen in time,
But within us,
Within us.
A living, changing presence,
Working through flesh and blood
and joy and tears.
What difference does it make?

Who art in HEAVEN…
Heaven was once
A faraway place
A distant hope
A bribe, even,
For good behaviour.
Until the great transgression,
The breaching of the boundary
Between God
And humanity.

Now God says, 'Heaven is within you
Where I make my home.
I am closer to you than the clothes you're wearing,

Closer to you than the skin you're in.
And when you become aware of it,
My kingdom will come
The power to see life transformed will come
And it will be forever
And ever
Amen.[1]

In his book, *The Great Spiritual Migration*, Brian D. McLaren, says this:

> 'For centuries, Christianity has been presented as a system of beliefs. That system of beliefs has supported a wide range of unintended consequences, from colonialism to environmental destruction, subordination of women to stigmatisation of LGBT people, anti-Semitism to Islamophobia, clergy paedophilia to white privilege. What would it mean for Christians to rediscover their faith not as a problematic system of beliefs, but as a just and generous way of life, rooted in contemplation and expressed in compassion, that makes amends for its mistakes and is dedicated to beloved community for all. Could Christians migrate from defining their faith as a system of beliefs to expressing it as a loving way of life? Could Christian faith lose the bitter taste of colonialism, exclusion, judgment, hypocrisy and oppression, and regain the sweet and nourishing flavour of justice, joy and peace?'[1]

I have critiqued elsewhere the common-sense notion of faith identity that McLaren describes.[2] Traditionally being Christian has meant assuming a God-given, pre-existent, definable corpus of teaching – let us call that 'doctrine', which a believing subject affirms or adopts – a process which we might call 'belief'. Once affirmed, this belief is then expressed in communal and individualised forms or religious activity: prayer, ritual, worship, social and political action, and so on. The dominant story about faith identity enmeshes us in a vicious triangle where doctrine, belief and expression are inextricably linked together, and have a linear connection. My use of the word 'vicious' stems from an awareness of the acute spiritual pain that can be felt when one finds oneself impaled on any of the three points of this triangle or, indeed, caught up in questions about how the three relate to one another. These experiences can feel like a strangulation of faith, and can leave one feeling a profound sense of alienation from one's spiritual roots. I want to explore these complex dynamics now, with a particular focus on gender and sexuality.

A Poem by Lydia

> There is "no place
> For me in the church
> Not even
> On its outermost edges"
> But still
> My knuckles rap
> Themselves raw
> On a door
> Of piety, so called
> And unpick belief
> Held far too tight, too sure
> Beat a beat
> That accompanies
> More than just my
> Grossly ill-perceived
> Borderland faith
> On the humble
> March home.

As McLaren says:

> 'When beliefs become a primary marker for belonging, religious gatekeepers gain one of humanity's greatest powers: to excommunicate or expel. In this way, belief-based systems centralise power and provide an easy way to test compliance with authorities: *will you recite the required beliefs*? Belief systems perform practical survival and political functions that are completely independent of the truth of their component beliefs. Believing, it turns out, is more about belonging and behaving – and more about politics and sociology – than we typically realise.'[3]

Many of us feel on a visceral level that faith should not be reduced to a tool of social control or political manipulation. As we saw in the last chapter, it should be a form of liberation; a way to connect with the source of our being – God, and with our sense of who we are called to be as unique individuals, loved unconditionally by that God.

I want to turn to queer theory to help us to model faith differently. To the extent that it has been on the agenda at all, the 'queering' of Christianity has tended to mean the process of making churches and Christian institutions (including church teaching) more amenable to participation by lesbian, gay, bisexual and transgendered people. But I want to use it in a slightly different way. After Eve Sedgwick,[4] I will use it to denote attempts to disrupt what have hitherto been considered necessary and common-sense alignments. In queer theory this disruption is of what are otherwise considered to be the self-evident and natural triad of biological sex, gender identity and sexual orientation. As Sedgwick points out, normatively speaking one's biological sex is used to read off a whole list of other personal characteristics: your self-perceived gender alignment; the biological sex, gender alignment and masculinity or femininity of your preferred partner; and your procreative choice, to name but a few. In exploring the notion of 'queer' she is interested in the possibilities that emerge when these normative alignments do not apply. As she puts it: 'That's one of the things that "queer" can refer to: the open mesh of possibilities, gaps, overlaps, dissonances and resonances, lapses and excesses of meaning when the constituent elements of anyone's gender, of anyone's sexuality aren't made (or can't be made) to signify monolithically.'[5]

To be clear about what she means, let's give an example. A baby is born. The common-sense assumption is that it will be a boy or a girl, and that this fact will be clear from the start: 'It's a girl!', or 'It's a boy!'. And from that moment (or, more probably, even before, since the biological sex of the child may have been disclosed by ultrasound), those who surround the baby will make decisions about how to treat that child based on its unambiguous biological sex: what colour clothing to buy; what kinds of toys; how to decorate the nursery. Many of these decisions will be subconscious; all will be largely driven by the values and assumptions of the child's wider social context. This we call the social construction of gender. And as the child grows up, so its gender identity will be refined and formed through its relationships with others within the family, at school and at play, and through their engagement with wider social forces including, now, social media. The male child is expected to become masculine (a man), and the female child is expected to become feminine (a woman). Integral to these binary identities is the assumption that to be a man or a woman is to choose those of the so-called 'opposite sex' to relate to sexually.

What Eve Sedgwick calls 'queer' is anything that disrupts these common-sense alignments and assumptions. This can mean many things. It may be that a baby is born not obviously male or female, but with sex characteristics that are ambiguous (they are intersex). Or from a very early age a child may have a deep sense that their gender identity does not fit with their physical sex (they are transgender). Or they may feel that neither gender category is one they can claim. They are both male and female or neither male nor female (they are 'gender queer'). It may be that as they grow they do not behave in ways that are considered socially acceptable for someone of their sex – for example they may be too 'masculine' for what is expected of a girl (a 'tomboy'), or too 'feminine' for what is expected of a boy ('effeminate'). Societies differ in terms of what is expected and acceptable behaviour for men and women in terms of gender, but all societies have limits and boundaries. And finally, a person may choose those of the non-prescribed gender to relate to sexually (they may be gay, lesbian, bisexual, or simply find that gender is not a defining criterion in determining their sexual attraction to another person). All these experiences involve what Sedgwick would call 'queering' the common-sense sex/gender narrative.

Let's take this definition of queer (the disruption of common sense alignments) into the sphere of faith by exploring the parallels between Sedgwick's 'sex, gender and sexual object choice' and the vicious triangle of doctrine, belief and expression. If I discover myself to be a lesbian, and have been brought up as a Christian, I may sense some dissonance with my faith tradition which I feel called to explore. In the process, I might study some theology and church history. And through that study I discover that various aspects of what I had been taught were pre-existent, divinely ordained aspects of the corpus of Christian teaching have actually been highly contested throughout Christian history, with people of faith taking a range of different perspectives. I might find that not only is this true of so-called 'second order' aspects of church teaching, but that it is also true of doctrines that are often taken to define Christianity's very essence: the divinity of Christ, the atonement and the Trinity, the authority of scripture. Next time a churchman tells me that lesbian sexuality is ruled out by church teaching and always has been, I will have cause to doubt the validity of his claim. But as I am only an individual and the corpus of doctrine is backed by considerable institutional power, I may perceive my beliefs to fall outside of the boundaries of traditional Christianity and therefore doubt the appropriateness of undertaking any Christian religious expression. In other words, doubt at the level of doctrine throws up uncertainty with regard to belief and expression that are supposed to flow, in a common-sense way, from it. This severely compromises any sense of belonging.

Or what if we start in a different place, with religious expression? In the previous chapter Rebecca spoke about her sense that she and her transgender partner could not express their love and commitment to one another as the people they are now in the context of the cathedral where they worship. Having been through the experience of her partner's transition, with all the changes and upheaval that involved, she says very clearly, '…we don't want to use their words. We are rejecting what the church offers at these important times of our lives because what they offer does not fit our narrative, or reflect how we want to be thought of or named.' This is a powerful expression of how her perception of the congealed doctrine and belief system of the establishment, which does not reflect her reality, thereby makes it impossible for her to fully embrace the forms of expression which flow from it. They do not 'fit'. So it is that, 'Every Sunday I go to church is a struggle', with the result that she and her partner share in a weekly Eucharist away from the institutional church with others who are 'living our lives counter to convention'.

In the book *Queer Theology*[6] Kathy Rudy writes from the position of someone who had her position as a scholar and teacher in a Divinity School taken from her as a result of her writing on sexism and homophobia being inextricably intertwined. She writes, 'For me…the entire world of faith and religion seemed tainted, filled with hurt, unwelcoming. This shift came for me not as a result of reasoned deliberation but rather as one of those life events where your emotions seem to reconfigure themselves, where the meaning of many things is altered, almost without your consent. I think of how these events organised my life into "before" and "after" frames.'[7]

The vicious triangle model of faith demands that one believes or doesn't, belongs or is an outsider. There is no middle way. But what many women need is precisely that: a middle way. As Kathy Rudy puts it, 'What I need is a theory of subjectivity that would allow me to be two contradictory things at the same time, that would allow me to say "I believe" and "I don't" in a way that does not require coherent explanation. I need a theory that will allow me to be fragmented, not as a temporary stopgap measure until I figure out where I will end up, but a theory that will allow me to understand myself as divided, now and forever. I need a model that does not obligate me to be only one, unified person, that does not rest its idea of subjectivity on Enlightenment individuality, that sees fragmentation as a natural state and not one to be worked through.[8]

Rudy is not alone in her need to embrace internal contradictions. In exploring this, I'd like to draw upon the insights of Judith Butler. In her essay 'Imitation and Gender Insubordination' she reflects upon the experience of going off to a conference to 'be a lesbian', and she says this: 'How is it that I can both "be" one, and yet endeavour to be one at the same time? When and where does my being a lesbian come into play, when and where does this playing at being a lesbian constitute something like what I am? To say that I "play" at being one is not to say that I am not one "really"; rather, how and where I play at being one is the way in which the "being" gets established, instituted, circulated and confirmed…it is through the repeated play of this sexuality that the "I" is insistently reconstituted as the lesbian "I".'[9] Later, focusing on gender identity, she says, 'There is no volitional subject behind the mime who decides, as it were, which gender it will be today. On the contrary, the very possibility of becoming a viable subject requires that a certain gender mime be already underway…gender is not a performance that a prior subject elects to do, but gender is performative in the sense that it constitutes as an effect the very subject that it appears to express. The denial of the priority of the subject, however, is not the denial of the subject; in fact, the refusal to conflate the subject with the psyche marks the psychic as that which exceeds the domain of the conscious subject. This psychic excess is precisely what is being systematically denied by the notion of a volitional "subject" who elects at will which gender and/or sexuality to be at any given time and place.'[10]

To help explain what Butler means, it might help to use the image of the paper dolls you may (if you are old enough, and your gender was constructed in that way) have played with as a child. These were plain people-shaped templates onto which you could clip a range of different faces and clothing choices, changing and switching them around. So it is with our assumptions about identity. We assume a pre-existing subject (the blank template doll), to which we then add on different characteristics of identity: they are male, tall, heterosexual, able-bodied, etc. What Butler is saying is that the template cannot be separated from the things that are clipped onto it. Imagine that the template only emerges as we begin to affix attributes to it. There is no pre-existing subject, for our subjectivity comes into being through the different kinds of identity we perform. This is philosophically a very different way of looking at things – a post-modern way, not an enlightenment way. It gives Kathy Rudy, and the rest of us, a different way forward.

For in the traditional model of Christian identity, described earlier, there is a volitional subject who assents to a particular corpus of theological propositions, and undertakes religious activities as an expression of those beliefs. As I have shown, the experiences of lesbians and other women of Christian heritage fit ill with this schema, as we discover that there are limits to what the volitional religious subject can do. We find that we cannot, for instance, renounce at will our religious identity. Kathy Rudy describes it very powerfully thus, 'I enjoy my new life in Women's Studies and the secular academy where being a lesbian is pretty much a non-issue and where I think I understand the rules of the game. Sometimes. I enjoy the feeling of being a whole, secular subject and enjoy projecting that wholeness into my future. Sometimes. Other times, I miss the church terribly, feel lost without the reconciling wholeness it once offered me. Other times, I notice religious impulses hidden deep inside me, almost as if they were located in my bones. My desire for God sometimes feels beyond my rational control. So what I really need, it occurs to me, is not simply an explanation that says, "I am a fragmented subject that is both religious and secular," but rather a three-dimensional theory that will sometimes allow me to be always and only secular, and other times will allow me to see myself as divided, fragmented, and perpetually confused.'[11] Judith Butler's concept of 'psychic excess' helps us to take account and make sense of the vagaries of desire and unconscious motivation as manifested in Rudy's experience. As Butler might have said, 'This psychic excess is precisely what is being systematically denied by the notion of a volitional subject who elects at will whether or not to be a Christian at any given time or place.'

Butler leads us to a model of faith as performative, that which is constituted as an effect of the spiritual practices we undertake, in all their diversity and creative manifestations. It is through this model, I believe, that religious agency can be restored. According to the old model, faith is something you have or do not have, rather than something you do or create. That is why traditional discourses around loss of faith almost always emphasise passivity: something got up and left me, as spirits and souls used to leave bodies in dualistic cosmologies. There was nothing I could do about it – it just happened. A queer model of faith enables us to, as I suggested in the first chapter, set aside the distress of life as supplicants, saying 'please', to embrace our agency as prophets and pilgrims building something new.

So our focus shifts. Now the question is not: on which side of the Christian/post-Christian divide do I stand? Have I lost faith or have I still got it? And whose judgement is that? Rather, the question is, how have I been constituted as a religious subject thus far, and what kind of spiritual person will I become in the future through the practices I perform – by the ways I choose to inhabit my faith? Or, to put it another way, going back to Judith Butler's first quote, how and where will I 'play' at being a Christian? As she might have written, 'To say I "play" at being a Christian is not to say that I am not one "really"; rather, how and where I play at being one is the way in which the "being" gets established, instituted, circulated and confirmed....it is through repeated play of this religious identity that the "I" is insistently reconstituted as the Christian "I".'

In summary, I believe that queer theory gives us the potential for a new model of faith identity that gives greater scope for spiritual agency, replacing the old all-or-nothing dualistic model with more complex and nuanced possibilities. We can hold contradictory feelings, integrate past and future emotional investments, and think about ways to exercise our prophetic and subversive activities into the future.

If Judith Butler helps us to disconnect and disrupt the believing subject and the nature of religious expression and their inter-relationship, it is another theorist, scientist and epistemologist, Donna Haraway, who helps us with the final part of the triad – the God-given, pre-existent and definable corpus of teaching, which I have called 'doctrine'. Reading Haraway's essay, 'Situated Knowledges', I was particularly struck by her reflections on the feminist project to de-objectify scientific discourse. She speaks of the search for, 'a strong tool for deconstructing the truth claims of hostile science, by showing the radical historical specificity, and so contestability, of every layer of the onion of scientific and technological constructions...'[12]. She argues that the traditional concept of 'scientific objectivity' is a con – a 'god trick'; an attempt to have infinite vision whilst taking no responsibility for any vision in particular. Her quest has close parallels with the process I described earlier of a lesbian who digs into the history of her faith, only to find a similar contestability of 'every layer of the onion' of so-called theological objectivity. As I have written elsewhere, doctrine is always somebody's doctrine, and belief is always somebody's belief. Doctrine is never innocent, but always political.[13] Supposedly 'objective' theology is the God-trick par excellence.

Haraway's strategy is to redefine objectivity such that, 'Only partial perspective promises objective vision.'[14] She asserts that, 'The alternative to relativism is not totalisation and single vision... the alternative to relativism is partial, locatable, critical knowledges sustaining the possibility of webs of connections called solidarity in politics and shared conversations in epistemology...'[15] What Haraway calls 'situated knowledge' has been usefully taken up in theology to develop 'situated theologies' – otherwise known as theologies of liberation. These theologies bring scripture and tradition into dialogue with our human experience, in a process of reflection from which emerge truths which reflect our contextual human reality – rather than abstract disembodied ideas. Liberation theologies have been developed by communities that feel ill-served by normative theology: Black men and women; people with disabilities; those who are economically marginalised; and queer people. As Pamela Lightsey puts it in her book on Womanist Queer Theology, 'Womanists have always believed that we come to know God by our experience of God. Therefore, from the writings of our founding womanist scholars, it has always been argued that theology, if it is to be efficacious, must be done from the context of the experience of the oppressed. In that vein, queer womanist theology proposes that any theology that does not respect the context of queer Black women has no purpose and is therefore dead. We have found the academy and Church to be reservoirs of dead theology that refused to drink from the liberating theological perspectives of any sources that were not derived by the status quo. And so they died of dehydration, unable to survive in our oasis of critical reflection, and are dead to us not because they failed to become experts of other theological particularities but because they failed at least to dip into our pools of thought. To put it bluntly, using the words of one contemporary African American woman featured on the Internet, "Ain't nobody got time for that!" '[16]

The message of liberation that emerges from paying attention to the experiences of Black queer women includes the following,

'It is because we have experienced and know God as love that Black queer womanists must dismiss as heretical any theology that purports that God gives us up to the powers of evil, and leaves us to fend for ourselves. Bishop Yvette Flunder, African American lesbian, said it well, "Church encourages self-loathing". But our experience with God – rather than how homophobic Black preachers have interpreted the text – demonstrates over and over again that God loves us just as we are, in our self-identity and in our living out that identity... We also know God as revealed to us in scripture. Queer Black Christian women believe *there is a word from the LORD*, indeed a *liberating* word from the LORD, and that that word can often be found in the Bible. We turn to the biblical witness with deep respect for its authoritative function in the churches and communities in which we worship and live.'[17]

Because they are based on the solid foundation of human experience, these situated theologies can articulate the complexity and nuances of our lives in a way that traditional theology cannot. And when brought together, they give the whole Christian community the gift of new insights about God that no one person alone can have. As Haraway puts it, they provide the 'possibility of webs of connections called solidarity in politics and shared conversations in epistemology.' So a Black man's experience of everyday racism may speak into a White lesbian's feelings of social marginalisation. A woman experiencing physical vulnerability through the deterioration of her health may articulate this in a way that makes sense of a gay man's sense of his own contested embodiment. And the God-talk that emerges from these specific and embodied conversations will generate truths about the divine which promise a rooted universality which is missing from our traditional theologies from nowhere, written by hidden someones.

Reflection

Was it something in her eyes that you saw? Some sense that a part of her was hiding; that she was hiding part of herself?

Imagine the excruciating humiliation of the woman caught, we are told, 'in the very act' of adultery. How was it to have an intimate and private moment (if that is what it was; if it was indeed consensual, an act of love, and not just an occasion of him helping himself. The him that is invisible in this story). If not, how much worse, as the private humiliation gave way to a public one. Shame declared for the consumption of all, to be stared at, vilified, threatened. Her life hanging in the balance. They were angry because she had transgressed. She had broken the rules, flouted the law, given in to her desires (if they were her desires). She had done what they would like to have done, and what they would like to have done to her. She excited their imaginations, their jealousies, their anger. Slag, slut, whore. She deserved to die and the law of Moses was on their side. Right was on their side, or so they thought.

You could read all this on their faces, hear it in their voices, their baying for so-called 'justice'. Justice for whom? And you made them wait. You had the authority to do that, and you used it. You denied them the power of setting the pace. You gave them a simple instruction, 'let the one who is without sin cast the first stone', and it turned everything upside down. Her humiliation became their embarrassment. Her fear, their loss of face. Her pain, their shame. They left.

Your empathy with her was astounding. You didn't look at her. You looked at the ground. You wrote in the sand. You saved her from one more male gaze. A simple but profound act of solidarity with one who was excluded, ridiculed and broken. How could you know how it felt to be her? And when her accusers had all gone, you offered her restoration. You gave her peace. Her transgression (if it was her transgression) was forgiven. You said, 'Go', and she could indeed go – where she wanted. She was not held then, not *restrained. No one could touch her. What did that feel like? What did she do with it?*

Perhaps you understood because you, too, transgressed. What was it like for you, Jesus, to be the only human being ever to cross the divide between God and humanity, to disrupt the cosmic order of things and change them forever? This was something you kept in the closet, revealing it, subtly and judiciously, to those who could take it in. To those who, at least in some small part, knew what transgression felt like.

Story

'And then I spotted her. A young, pretty woman walking towards me, dressed simply in jeans and t-shirt, with long straight brown hair, moving with the simplicity and ease of someone who does not have to think about who she is. She seemed, to my anxious eyes, utterly whole, utterly relaxed – body and soul moving as one. The very opposite of me. I remember thinking, "It is so easy for her." I remember feeling that she was who I wanted to be. She was how I wanted to be. I remember her coming towards me and smirking. She didn't laugh. Our eyes met for the briefest moment and she smirked.'[18]

We have seen how new models of faith identity can emerge from a process of 'queering' (that is disrupting) common sense connections. As Cheng says in his book, *Radical Love* '…queer theology can be understood as a theological method that is self-consciously transgressive, especially by challenging societal norms about sexuality and gender. Thus, queer theology refers to a way of doing theology that, in the words of the Magnificat, brings down the powerful and lifts up the lowly. In particular, this theology seeks to unearth silenced voices or hidden perspectives'.[19] Likewise in the introduction to his *Queer Theology* collection, Gerard Loughlin says, 'To name theology as queer in this sense is to invoke "queer" as the strange or odd, the thing that doesn't fit in... Queer seeks to outwit identity. It serves those who find themselves and others to be other than the characters prescribed by an identity. It marks not by defining, but by taking up a distance from what is perceived as the normative. The term is deployed in order to mark, and to make, a difference, a divergence.'[20]

In deploying this queer theology, though, we need to take account of its costliness, and reflect on the spiritual significance of that. A life of transgressing boundaries and norms is a challenging life, not a comfortable one, and this makes such lives fertile crucibles for new theological truths. *Dazzling Darkness*, by Rachel Mann, is a startling example of how revelatory insight about God can be wrought from the agony of Gethsemane, including her experience, as a trans woman, of transitioning. I would therefore like to quote her at some length. She says,

> 'There is truly something extraordinary, horrifying and painful, in identity terms, about being "caught between". It is a land of shadows, of twilight, and sometimes of almost complete darkness. Perhaps many of us have had that kind of experience in some form or other – the experience of unemployment, say – but the trans person's experience can represent its very acme...Attention-seeker that I am, the last thing I wanted during that time of androgyny, was to be noticed – and to be laughed at and pilloried – for looking "in-between."...I still sometimes dream of that transitioning time of ambiguity and it has the character of a nightmare. It became so clear to me that what freaked others out and, indeed, freaked me out was the convention-breaking power of androgyny and of indeterminacy. Being "in-between" deprived those who looked upon me of ready-made, and mostly unquestioned, gender dimorphic categories – that is, of the unspoken visual assessment that "x" is male or female. The simple fact is that we live in a culture that is conditioned

to look for the "either/or" rather than the "both/and" or the "not quite".[21]

The pain of being 'in between' comes in part from the fact that those who inhabit liminal space are holding up a mirror to everybody else, inviting them to acknowledge that the foundations of their own identities: the taken-for-granted, unquestioned aspects of their nature, whether that is masculinity, femininity or heterosexuality, are not as natural as they might think. It is a profoundly unsettling insight that who you are is, in many ways, an accident, and could easily have been otherwise. It is not to your credit and it is not your fault. What you do with your identity is something for which you are responsible, and for which you can be held to account. This can be profoundly scary for those in socially dominant groups who have never questioned their entitlements because they have never needed to. The result is a kind of collective punishment of those who, simply by living out who they are, call into question the complacency and unexamined nature of dominant identities.

Yet to undertake the journey of discovery into the depth of one's identity can be transformative, not just for the person doing it, but for all those who are willing and open to learning the lessons that emerge.

> 'To feel as if one is losing one's agency and self, indeed feeling like one has become a kind of non-person, is uncomfortable and something most of us quite reasonably avoid. And yet it is revealing. At a head level – a level that genuinely matters to me as a thinker and intellectual searcher – there is simply no doubt that the experience of being "in-between" reveals, in a truly visceral way, the extent to which our gender and sexual categories are constructed and are, in an important sense, arbitrary. I am not suggesting that these categories don't matter nor that simply through "Living as x" makes one a man or a woman. There is such a thing as an inner dimension to being a man or a woman. But there is simply no doubt that

there is a huge performative dimension to who we are, shaped unconsciously from birth and which many people do not like having their attention drawn to. Part of the reason the gender ambiguous disturb many people is because they expose reality: rather than being like hard and fast mathematical laws, our identities – our human practices, behaviours, beliefs and so on – are more like sediment thrown down on a river bed. This sediment runs very deep in places and is almost impossible to dislodge, but in others it is laid more thinly.'[22]

There are similarities here with the experiences of many lesbian and gay people over the past few decades – the sense that simply by being gay and relating to someone of the same gender, you are somehow calling into question the very legitimacy of heterosexuality. This is, at least in part, the dynamic behind the opposition amongst Christians to equal marriage. Some suggest that if two men or two women can get married, this somehow undermines the 'specialness' of opposite sex marriage. James Alison calls this, 'the gay thing'. This, he says:

> '…is something which has just happened, and is just happening, to all of us, whatever our own sexual orientation is. You can be as straight as you like, but being straight is no longer the same as it was when there was no such thing as "gay." Our picture of what it is to be male or female has undergone, and is undergoing, huge changes which affect us not only from without, but from within. We find ourselves relating, whether we want to or not, with each other, and with ourselves, in new ways as a result of something which is far bigger than any of us and which is just happening.'[23]

To complete the parallel, we could say about trans issues, 'You can be as cis as you like, but the fact is that you would never have been called, or called yourself, cis, if the reality of transgender people had not erupted into public awareness. The fact that it has means that none of us can see our gender identity in the same way again.'

For all of these reasons, it is agonising to be the person who personifies and represents all of this contestation. But for Rachel Mann, the pain of it reveals something new and revolutionary for her, and for all of us, about the nature of God:

> 'My moving into the world of ambiguity and the "in-between" was a stepping away from self, into death and darkness. It was also a stepping into "Otherness". That is, I took upon myself what is sometimes known as "the Other": the one who is most definitely not seen as belonging to the dominant or normative groups and so can be dismissed as less than fully human, or stereotyped as a "threat". It is a profoundly uncomfortable place to be, especially if one has a huge desire to belong. But much as I could not live it again, I now reckon that period as a kind of gift. A dark, uncomfortable gift. But a gift nonetheless. A gift from the dark, living God.'[24]

The theological vision we are glimpsing is amazing. It has profound parallels with what God did in Jesus – traversing the boundary to become God on earth; the suffering servant, the man of sorrows – acquainted with the grief of inhabiting the ultimate liminality. Enabling the 'otherness' of God to be encountered by human beings, then incorporated by us into our identities as children of God. In words which take us back to the poem with which we began this chapter, Rachel Mann speaks of her discovery of,

> '…God at her most intimate – the one who simply is when all else seems lost. This is God beyond doctrine and without boundaries. This is God beyond reason and the uses we would make of her… We cannot use her: she comes in her own time and meets us when we have nothing else left. And all she is is love. She is not comfort, but the thinnest thread holding you above despair. This is not a God we can summon up for

ourselves and for our own purposes…This is God in all her stark love – stripped of sentiment and our manipulations; the God who holds crucifixion and death in her depths.'[25]

Chapter Six

Remaking Love

Reflection

Another woman would have pleaded with him not to go through with it; would have wanted to save herself the excruciating pain of losing her beloved. But not you. You chose, simply, to accompany him. To walk with him, eyes wide open, into the valley of the shadow of death. You felt the powerlessness, the pain of betrayal, and the sense of injustice at a trial that was a travesty. It was just one more example of political pragmatism working itself out to protect the powerful – that unholy alliance of those who otherwise were bitter enemies – the rulers of state and the rulers of faith.

How did you survive it? You had a resilience, for sure, the inner strength of a survivor – of one who had faced down her own humiliations and near-death experiences. So in a way this was familiar territory, but in another sense it wasn't at all. You would have known how to deal with the pain if they had been torturing you; how to dissociate from what they were doing to your body; how to block out the manipulation of your mind. You would have contained that pain in the ways you had perfected. But this wasn't you, it was him. It was Jesus, the man you loved. You had to suffer it as he suffered it. This pain was a mountainous presence that couldn't be moved, or got round, or overcome. All you could do was face it. Every blow struck home with you; every whiplash burned; every insult cut deep; every slice of him they took was taken from you also. And you watched him let it happen. Silently, he went through with it. Then he was gone. He had left you, alone.

Could it really have happened? Somehow you couldn't take it in, so afterwards you went to be with him – to be close to his precious body bound as it was now with ointment and wrappings. But when you got to the tomb he had vanished. His body was all that you had left of him, and somebody had stolen that too. How could they do that, after everything else they had put him through? You wept with despair and bewilderment, and for the massive tearing loss that ripped through you all over again.

You loved him but you knew you couldn't hold him. Your bodily connection with him would be temporary, you were sure, but you were just as sure that your spiritual connection would endure. How could it be otherwise, when he had given you your life back? You always knew this was – had to be – an 'open palmed' kind of love; that something like this would happen. He belonged elsewhere, and to someone else.

In the midst of this a stranger came, and asked you why you were crying. You would have ignored him but for the fact he might have known where Jesus was. Then suddenly you heard him. He said your name in that way he had of calling you out of and into yourself. 'Mary', he said. And everything changed. In that moment you realised it was still him, though he looked different – transformed, somehow. Who was he now? What was the new meaning of him? You desperately wanted to hold him, and you reached out. But gently, he said, 'Do not cling to me'. You knew then that this was not a reversal of history – not a rolling back of the last three days, but that things had changed for ever. What you didn't yet know was what that meant.

So far in this book we have found out about our historical context: some of the key changes that have taken place over the past few decades. We have found out about the power structures that surround us – the many and various forms of oppression and silencing that we resist as women, especially within Christian traditions. And we have found out how creative, inventive and improvisational we can be in response, particularly in recreating our spiritual lives. Now we come to an exploration of how we live out our relationships – our intimacies and commitments, given that we are not well served by the conventional life patterns and inflexible expectations foisted upon us by a heteronormative world.

Culture Matters

Our first recognition must be that we embody the value system that we have imbibed from our social context. We are host to a constant inner dialogue between our personal feelings, our intellectual opinions and the voices of 'the world' that live within us. These voices are powerful and they manifest themselves viscerally. They operate at a gut-level, and that is where the resistance is also borne. Racism, sexism, heterosexism – and the wider value systems about what makes for physical beauty, worldly success and failure, and what makes us loveable, acceptable and worthy, are carried in our embodied hearts and minds. Recalibration of our values and redemption from negative and damaging messages about who we are need to happen at multiple levels within ourselves. This inner transformation will be an ongoing task, and is as much a spiritual practice as it is an intellectual and emotional one.

Vivienne

'When I fell for someone else, I flagellated myself for it. How can I want someone with every part of me, when I am married to another? I haven't been able to pray about it. It's made me question God. Why am I in love with two people? If I was a man in another part of the world I could be in love with two people.

I went to talk to my vicar about it and he was wonderful. At the end of the conversation I dropped in something that had happened to me with men when I was four, five and nine years old.

Inappropriate things that adult men did to me. Do I have a weird relationship with sex because of that? Is this how you get people to like you? Maybe I don't know what the boundaries are? I feel a massive sense of judgement, and I don't know if I believe in God.'

Martha

'When I was growing up I experienced a series of powerful attractions to women – always a bit older than myself. So imagine this: me on the school hockey field at fifteen. It was a winter afternoon. I was part of the team of those who weren't really very good at hockey. I liked that group. My main reason for being there, though, was that *she* was the teacher. I took any opportunity to be near to her, in her sights. Miss Brown. Her. How to describe what I felt for her? She took up most of my head-space for the best part of six years. From the age of fourteen, when she came, as a young teacher, to the school, to the age of twenty when we started to make the successful transition from unbalanced devotion on my part, to equal friendship between the two of us. That blessed time when to call her by her first name became easy and natural. Miss Brown transformed into first-name terms. I – we, I guess – worked hard to achieve that. She was also my Religious Studies teacher. Four periods a week, plus the hockey. But it wasn't enough. When I was anywhere near her, I was never relaxed. It was partly because of her that I studied religion. She brought spiritual questions to life for me. She made me think about meaning; made me think about value; made me feel joy and pain; enabled me to feel God; made me question everything I thought I knew about who I was and what I wanted out of life. She influenced me in so many ways. Scary the power she had. I didn't know I was in love. I certainly didn't know it had anything to do with my sexuality. That was unimaginable.

Back to that hockey field. The game was over. We were walking back up the hill to school. This was my weekly chance to walk next to her. Just for a few minutes. I looked around at everyone else and thought, "They're not even thinking about it, about her. Not giving her a second thought. Just walking." Part of me wished I could be free of whatever these feelings were, and be like them. Normal, unconcerned. One time, I made a joke. She laughed. I *loved it* that I could do that sometimes. Make her laugh. Affect her. Then she reached out and touched the back of my neck. A light touch, in jest, that's all it was, but for me it was the most powerful and unforgettable tactile gesture of my life. I was speechless, breathless, light-headed. It was bitter-sweet, gut-wrenching, intense pleasure and pain mixed together. I didn't know what to do, didn't know what to think. I didn't know what this made me and didn't know whether I cared. I had no words for this and I wasn't sure I wanted any. Certain words hovered, but I didn't let them take shape because I sensed danger in them. I loved this woman, and I was afraid.'

*

Vivienne breaks the affectional 'rules' that go with being married. You are not supposed to fall in love with another, when you have promised total love and commitment to your spouse. She punishes herself for feelings that she cannot help or control, whilst at the same time recognising that the rules themselves are culturally specific – other societies in other parts of the world have structures for this eventuality. We don't. Her assumption is that these feelings are somehow the result of damaging and painful things that have happened to her, not that they could be a gift. She is thrown off course, to the extent that she feels judged and found wanting, and ultimately doubts God.

In Martha's experience, there is a sense of hesitation, fear, and simply not seeing what is dazzlingly obvious. She lives with a maelstrom of intense feeling but is disqualified, by seemingly invisible and incomprehensible forces, from naming her attraction and love. She was unable to feel what she was really feeling because, culturally speaking, it was not possible for her to be 'one of them', a woman who falls for other women – a lesbian. Uttering the 'L' word, even only to herself, was simply too frightening. In identity terms, she could not afford to let her feelings be real.

Whatever progress has been made in social attitudes and political moves towards equality, being lesbian is still about an 'absence'. Because it is an unsayable word, a stigmatised cultural category – a word of abjection and horror; a taboo, the impact of naming oneself in line with one's feelings has, for many women, physical embodied consequences until, at gut level, we come to terms with it. These powers of abjection cannot be as easily erased as practical forms of discrimination. They are carried in our collective psyche and live on. The effects of this may be manifested in the form of eating too little or too much; drinking too much; experiencing physical stress and sometimes depression and anxiety. They are ameliorated by finding networks and communities that generate a sense of belonging – spaces where we have no need to translate our experience and our reality into foreign cultural languages.

As we work out how to live our relational lives, we need to address the question of what other visceral value systems are at work in us as we pick our way through our attractions and commitments. This applies to all of us, whatever our sexuality. Who do we expect to love, and what happens when love visits us outside of our expectations? What kinds of bodies attract us and why? What colour skin? What gender, what kinds of intelligence and creativity? How does the reality of loving challenge these textures of the culture that lives in us – and how does it feel to embody that challenge in the deepest parts of ourselves?

Power Matters

The things that texture our psyches work themselves out in systems and structures. However tempting it may be to assert simply that there is 'neither black nor white, male nor female, gay or straight', but that we are 'all just people', in the real world this is not credible, for it takes no account of those power structures and systems, and it does nothing to subvert them. And if we are seeking justice, we need to subvert them.

Think about the *power* of doing the 'right thing'; of *being* the 'right thing'. Notice the systems of social reward and punishment. Remember feeling comfortable in the wake of cultural approval ('getting' your first boyfriend as a teenage girl – proving somebody wants you, that you are pretty and desirable); relive the vulnerability of being on the receiving end of cultural opprobrium (the only unpartnered kid at the school disco). Those who are gay or lesbian and have spent decades attending heterosexual weddings whilst being unable to marry or demonstrate their relational commitments in public will know what I mean. They will have felt the inner conflict of being happy for their friends on a joyous occasion, whilst simultaneously experiencing an acute sense of being locked out of privilege; ultimately teaching themselves not to want it. White people with Black partners, and Black people with White partners will also know what I mean. They will have experienced many weird and painful dynamics. For example, the passive-aggressive possessiveness that many White men have for White women, and the subtle and not-so-subtle ways that they express it. The racism manifesting itself as a 'desire for the exotic other' that many White women feel towards Black men, that manifests itself as bitterness and jealousy when a Black man doesn't choose them. And when we notice these things and call them out, we will have been told we are being hypersensitive, making a fuss about nothing, or have a 'chip on our shoulders'. We live in a system that punishes and rewards according to its own conventions. Conventions that, as people of justice, we cannot and should not own.

Those of us who are, in some way, 'queer', using the word as I did in Chapter Five, live on the underside of the power of these conventions. For lesbians and trans women, for instance, our very being is delegitimised and called into question. We have a right to *be* only insofar as the power structures allow it. And the really clever thing is how hidden this is. Society takes away your full right to be, whilst asserting, in explicit terms, that you still have it. And it hides it so subtly and successfully that those not on the underside of power find it almost impossible to see that this has happened, and even harder to see their part in it.

Some of us have experienced both sides of the acceptability divide in terms of our personal relationships. We have been perceived to be both gay and straight at different times and through different relationships. When living a legitimated life (e.g. apparently heterosexual), one notices the rewards and comfort that flow from that position. This, in turn, enables us to sense more clearly its absence. You see with clarity how the system rewards or rewarded you when you understand from experience how the punishment works. Resistance is our modus operandi when we live on the underside of power. It gives us insight into systems of power and privilege, and possibilities of alliance-building with others similarly located.

Unnamed Loves Matter

Audre Lorde, the African American womanist warrior poet who died in 1993, said this, 'Every woman I have ever loved has left her print upon me, where I loved some invaluable piece of myself apart from me – so different that I had to stretch and grow in order to recognise her. And in that growing, we came to separation, that place where work begins. Another meeting.'[1]

Every human encounter is an invitation to go deeper; to embrace the challenge of difference and be changed. One cultural value we live with is the tendency to over-emphasise the importance of one, singular, partnered relationship. That applies to the gay world and the straight. It marginalises those with no spouse or partner, obviously, but it does more than that. It encourages us to devalue so many of our other deep connections – usually with the word 'just'. 'Oh, don't worry about him, he's just a friend'.

We each have, potentially if not actually, a vast hinterland of passionate connections that make up the rest of our relational lives, once the question of whether we are partnered or not is answered. The paucity of our language in this regard interests me. For naming is power, and we have very few names for those we love who are not spouses or blood relatives. Think about your experience. Who are those on whom your life depends; without whom you would be bereft; those who have made you who you are, and those who still do. They may be people you share passionate interests with, or those with whom you have creative partnerships. You may share a deep spiritual connection. These relationships may or may not be conventionally 'sexual', but they involve our sexuality because we are whole people within them. These are those with whom we are bold, take risks, make ourselves vulnerable. These relationships have no name. They are often pushed aside, in the conventional pecking order of priorities, by the contractual, the legitimate, the defined. Yet they are always bursting into and through relational spaces and gaps – sometimes chaotically, reminding us of the mystery of love; its giftedness, its unpredictability. If love is of God, how could it be otherwise?

Sometimes people simply erupt into our lives, and we are never the same again. We could see these people as gifts from God – often gifts that we didn't know we needed, and weren't looking for. They just show up and start asking questions that somehow go to the heart of who we are in God, help us explore our doubts and fears, our difficulties in feeling loved and being loved. These are relational gifts that leave us feeling cherished, known, recognised and cared for. We could call such people 'Soul friends'.

If love is of God, we must embrace this hinterland; work with the grain of it. Not allow the world to tell us that these connections that have no name have no importance. On the contrary, we must work to articulate them better, to develop a language for them, to explore how to live with them authentically, ethically and with integrity. I am not suggesting the development of a more complex labelling and classification system for different shades of relationship. I am pointing us to an Audre Lorde-inspired poetic for nuanced self-expression.

Lydia

'I have fallen in love with love. Love is not a fixed thing or a commodity. It's about allowing erotic connection, through the body, harnessing the power of it. The question is how to make sense of it, how to navigate it, how to discern where to go with it?

Still, if you are a woman, there are certain ways you are expected to behave. To be part of a group there are conditions of identity. If you are too fluid, if you are open to what may come, you can't win. I don't want to be pretty. I want to be beautiful in a way that God enjoys me. I don't see "men" and "women", I see the energy of a person. I have both within myself, and the different poles can come out at different times.

There are all sorts of tensions around in trusting one's desire. How to do it, but not be naïve? How to be open to a spirit of exploration, but not be exploited? To be able fully and really to love another you have to be receptive, but not exploitative. There are many things we don't do, relationally, because we are afraid. What do we aspire to? What does it mean "to be together" with someone else? Fidelity is very important to me, but it must be possible to be faithful, whilst also allowing love to flow where it will. I wrote a poem called 'Love Itself' to explore how, when we are dealing with these love energies, in concrete terms these forces cannot be contained. We're in a different order of reality. There is just an opening and a channelling of Godly love – the thing itself. For me, this has held true. Here is a part of the poem:

> Save me from religious visions,
> heroic missions and creeds
> divisive when intoned.
> Let me welcome Love

unto my breast
where prayers are heard
and find their rest
in the heart that is soul's home.
Women and Men are sacred gifts
who tread this path alone
but dream and search
for Zion's bliss
communion's holy ground
where pain is gone
and dread is dead
and fear, no longer known.
It is Love itself our duty is
To delve ever deeper into beauty, hid
To proclaim Love's triumph on cross and altar
And in our passion, ne'er to falter
It is Love itself who calls
when into another's arms we fall
the desire in their eyes
is our nature recognized
We must heed the call
and dare to fall
Honour the trust that has
been placed in us –
It is meet and right so to do
and to do any other is
to betray a God of Love,
our Lover…

and…

They'll smite me,
they'll smite me for this
a discipleship so unruly, unrehearsed.
No authority granted,

and none sought,
Only inner battles ceaselessly fought.
No footsteps to follow
No hand to hold
No truths to tell
and none to be told
Only a heart that is
a cavern for mystery
in which Love itself unfolds…

And…

It is Love itself for which I long
to live, to write, to speak
But it is Love itself demands of me
that I do nothing
except let It flow, and
allow my broken heart to beat.'

And Lydia's story continues:

'At one time I had two options open to me – to live in a polyamorous community in Germany, or to join a convent. To some people these might look like opposites, but to me they are not at all. I have a sense that I want to be devoutly religious and pure, but also I don't want to deny anything within myself. I thought that I wanted to become a nun so somebody could tell me that I'm pure, and to have a life that's structured around finding the purity. I think that's why, in the end, I wrote my own interpretation of monastic vows to express my own understanding of them:

Poverty is a positive reaction to excessive consumption. It is also the cause of avoidable misery and unnecessary suffering. To choose it is to cry out against inequality but not truly to understand it. It has little to do with money and everything to do with how you count your blessings and measure your successes.

Chastity is a learning to wait, a command to consider fully your desires, not a prohibition against acting on them. It has little to do with sex and masturbation and everything to do with what motivates your desires, if only to help put you in touch with the source of your erotic longing that requires no correction. It dovetails with your preparedness to take responsibility for the consequences of your actions and your commitment to learning the lessons of its mystery, humble within the knowledge that you'll never get it exactly "right" and you may often be "wrong". It is not a marriage per se, nor an eye for an eye, not a sacrament ipso facto that requires you to stilt your growth in order to preserve fidelity to its earthly covenant. It is not a command to suffer in lieu of love, life, laughter and learning. It is the trinity living within your body and connecting you to your soul through your wanting to share in the perichoresis of life's dance.

Obedience is a question of authority that you must never cease to ask. It involves honesty and self-examination of the most painful kind. It requires courage enough to speak truth to power and to suffer the consequences. It demands a will submitted to a higher principle and yet an entirely personal investment in what is being sacrificed. It will never ask of you to lie. (A lie being a grievous sin and not a withholding of your full truth, a reframing of it that renders it a kinder offering.) It will never ask you to betray what feels right. It will stay alongside you day and night until you align your choices with the God inside. Forgiving you, if you wholeheartedly desire it to, in the meantime.

Perhaps it's helpful also to say all this, again, poetically:

Phantom Lovers

As the night recedes, reveals its treasure
Your soul pours over me and in you, mine
Before daylight reality defines
My spirit flees its moral mind, escapes
Escapes to be with you, your mortal flesh

Worships beauty with rapturous pleasure
Returns to dress the wounds of want, to grieve
To pray away the sin, imagined deed.
They say I'm a witch, untrustworthy type
But to you my Prince I remain in sight
You are a faithful man and I am chaste
Let us love with passion, not love with haste
For Phantom Lovers are often despised
By those who see not the Divine's disguise.'

*

Lydia shows how living beyond ethical strictures imposed by external authorities is far from the much feared 'anything goes' approach to relational ethics. Thin ends of wedges, slippery moral slopes and the spectre of moral chaos are all laid before us by those who take an authoritarian approach to sexuality; those who say they know what God wants for humanity; that it is the same for everyone, and that they have privileged access to the truth of that. Our role, they say, is to take it on trust that the Truth has been revealed to them, that their interpretation of that truth is correct, and to do as we are told. Yet as women and as queer people we have no reason to trust, for these approaches have not trusted us, or our experience. Rather, they have served only to oppress and abuse us, with no accountability. We know that authoritarian heteronormativity would obliterate our lived experience if it could.

By contrast, Lydia embraces a self-aware and reflexive approach to desire, and in her response to it a determination to avoid exploitation of any kind. She wants to be accountable to others, to herself and to God, with whom she maintains a constant internal conversation. She identifies God as the source of our erotic longings, and the one who invites us to undergo the spiritual and personal growth which those longings pull us towards. She does not suggest for one moment that this is an easy path but one of integrity and challenge, demanding courage.

Authoritarian approaches speak from outside our experience, and address us in a register that is discordant to us. Demands that lesbian and gay people 'be it but don't do it', or that we be 'celibate' – and, a new trend, use of the phrase 'same sex attracted' as though our feelings for others are somehow separate from other aspects of who we are, make no sense to us. If it wasn't for their political power; the fact that such attitudes are determinative of church policies on sexuality, we could simply ignore them and leave them to one side. But for some, lives and careers are shaped by these distorted understandings of our sexuality. We have therefore been wise to construct new and alternative meanings, in a different register that harmonises with our reality.

Nel and Megan

'They arrive together, in an orange van. The wedding colours are diverse: bold purples, greens and yellows. Sunflowers, woodland and straw bales are the backdrop to the ceremony. Creator God is at the heart; the wedding guests sit in a circle of friendship and love. A reading asks: can you be with pain? can you be with joy? The words of friends and family affirm about Nel and Megan that, "we love them; we are with them; we are for them".

Megan says to Nel, "I will be your closest friend, confidante and partner for the rest of your life. With you I feel alive, at rest and free. With you I feel safe, cared for and protected, loved, listened to, and trusted, able to grow, to try, to make mistakes, to let go, to be myself. With you I feel precious and beautiful. Life is more colourful with you. You are funny and wise and strong. The most fragile of hearts…it's easy to see God in you."

Nel says to Megan, "Precious soul-mate, you are someone to share laughter with, to grieve with, to deepen faith with. You have changed me. When I am not with you I feel homesick for nowhere. You teach me how to love myself. Silence with you is the most comforting place. Thank you for having the courage to be yourself. Thank you for waiting for me." '

*

Recently I was privileged to be part of a blessing of the marriage of two women. It was immensely moving, not least because the vulnerability of one of those women was such that the unconditional love she had found in her female partner had, I suspect, saved her life. The lesbian congregation sang, with great gusto and many tears, Charles Wesley's, 'Love Divine'. Written over 250 years ago, it was made for the occasion: 'Love divine, all loves excelling, joy of heaven, to earth come down…', then, 'Jesus thou art all compassion, pure, unbounded love thou art; visit us with thy salvation; enter every trembling heart.'

There has been a fear within the lesbian and gay community – perhaps particularly amongst lesbians – that equal marriage will lead to our absorption and appropriation by the heterosexual world. That the complex and fruitful negotiations of who we are to one another will be short-circuited if we inadvertently adopt heterosexual binary models of relationship. Nel and Megan's wedding ceremony, and the one deploying a subversive reading of Charles Wesley are indicative, I hope, of a different likely outcome of equal marriage. Queer people have had to 'be' another way, relationally speaking, for many reasons. For instance, if our social networks are minorities ones, these communities can be small. Lovers breaking up can threaten the cohesiveness of those communities, so we have developed ways of containing the potential disruption that relational break-ups can bring. There has been a blurring of the boundary between lovers and friends in a way that has been, traditionally, less possible for straight people. Lovers become friends, and friends become lovers. Lovers break up, but often remain friends. Strong networks can exist which give us mutual support as an alternative to, though more often now in addition to, that offered by our blood families. We need to find ways of ensuring that the richness of these ways of being and relating are woven into, not erased by, inclusion into the dominant social model of marriage.

Rebecca

'It suddenly struck me that my partner's coming out as transgender has enabled me to articulate my own sexuality as a lesbian, but I haven't done anything with that. I have got so much work still to do. My family and church background was such that we didn't talk about sexuality at all. I had no language for it. I realise now that I was attracted to the femininity in my partner. It was my first relationship, and my only relationship experience has been with her, and it has been difficult to know what my sexuality is because when we married she identified most closely as a gay man. Have I ever had a relationship with a man? Have I ever had a relationship with a woman? I find Jo Ind's writing[2] very helpful because she talks about defining our sexuality differently, according to what turns us on, not the gender of the person. For me physical movement is very important. There are only two men I have ever been attracted to. Both were tall, slim, dancers, gentle and in touch with their bodies. I've always known about that, but the evangelical church I was brought up in discouraged me from paying attention to it, saying that the most important relationship is with God and to maintain the furrow you are stuck in in relationship to that God.

I have been in a place of suffering, paradox, contradiction and incongruity, and I know that the divine works in me to change and shape and transform me, to lay aside my egoic self. Staying in our marriage was not always easy, and it was not what the institutional church wanted, but it has had its own blessings. I am a different person now: far preferable to the person I was. It has made me more compassionate and open. We all have challenges to work with. Being in another relationship, I would just have run up against it in a different way. Our marriage vows were significant in holding us together and re-creating what this was for six or seven years.

There was anger and a sense of feeling trapped. I was also very aware of the fragility of my partner's mental health. I stayed in the hope of growth and change once we were through the trauma years – I stayed to see where we would grow up. These days I probably wouldn't feel the obligation to marry.'

*

There is very little in Rebecca's marriage that would be recognised or encompassed by the traditional marriage narrative of the church. This was never a conventional 'romance' between a woman and a man who perceived the other to be a person of the 'opposite sex', complementing them and making them whole – becoming their 'other half'. The faithfulness and the commitment through change and trauma are deep, but they are wrought through a lonely process of working things out as they go along. As Rebecca says, her faith gave her no language for understanding her own sexuality or for negotiating the complexity of her relationship with her transgender spouse as it unfolded. She knows, though, that God has worked within her to change her. I suggest that what she has discovered about God represents precious 'gold dust' insight. We all need to learn from it. How will we hear it?

Change and Loss Matter

There is one final deep-seated cultural value that I would like to explore. We find it manifested particularly strongly within the Christian community. It is the assumption that permanence and stability in relationships are to be valued above all else. I am not arguing against these things as relational 'goods'. Megan's promise that she would be Nel's closest friend, confidante and partner for the rest of Nel's life is clearly life-giving and liberating, and the commitment to a safe and secure space where both partners can grow is something to which many people aspire. But the hegemony of the language of 'permanent, faithful and stable' as the assumed norm for heterosexual marriage and therefore, by extension, the criteria by which all sexual relationships are deemed acceptable, hides other realities.

It hides the fact that transitory and transient relationships are not worthless. With or without sex, short-term relationships can be crucial to us, and can reveal important truths about who we are. Even one-off conversations and encounters can change our lives. It also hides the fact that stability is not what it may seem. In the situation of an apparently 'permanent, faithful, stable' partnership, you have an interaction between two constantly changing people, with others coming into their orbit – sometimes remaining there and changing the relational dynamic, sometimes fading out. There will be losses as well as the birth of new things. Sometimes mutual growth is impossible, or the growth of one person – if it is to happen – will be at the expense of the other. In which case the partnership may need to end. Our culture traditionally deems such endings as failures, whereas they might be the best and most advisable outcome for all concerned. How do we honour, mark, and talk about that? How do we affirm what was good and life-giving whilst also recognising the value in moving on?

One thing that emerges from trans experiences is the value of change and transition and transformation. Speaking of his research into the experiences of trans people of faith, Chris Dowd says, 'Trans people do not change gender, they become the person they were meant to be. There is a sacrament of becoming. It is a spiritual quest, not a medical intervention. Transitioning is only the means to start constructing who you are meant to be, whatever medical stuff is done.' And he continues,

> 'Many things are born with the purpose of being transformed. God transforms people and things in order to show a truth, to show that transformation is sacred. The challenge is to forgive yourself, others and God; to move from rigidity to openness; to hold onto our love of God and remain convinced

that God is loving. For trans people going through this sacred transformation there is enormous spiritual growth. A lot of people have gone through some extremely difficult things in their personal relationships: separation; apparently forcing choices on others because they themselves felt they had no choice. All the evidence shows that children know between the ages of two and four that they are transgender, and they learn to hide it as a means of survival. Imagine what that means. They learn to hide, even sometimes from themselves because, unlike many ancient societies, we don't have a place for those of a third or fourth gender. We have no place for ambiguity. And the church is the custodian of the rigid binary gender myth which is why it is so ruthlessly imposed. If we let go of the gender myth, the church loses power. For the sake of trans people, and many others who don't fit, we need to dismantle the gender myth. We need a new meta-narrative that fits who we are and where we are. We need to simply communicate to people that "You are enough".

The transition and transformation that trans people model highlights something that is true for all of us. There is a mystery in what God wants for us. Our calling is to a pilgrimage of becoming the best that we can be; to becoming who we should be. There is a compelling pull to becoming who we are meant to become, in God. It is disruptive, unpredictable. It is not always friendly to the church's desire to keep everything under control and in the right place.

If we are called to transition and transformation, this will sometimes involve leaving others behind. Making a commitment to one path inevitably means closing others down. We will all experience times when it feels as though a sword has pierced our hearts because we cannot have what we want, or who we want, in the way that we want. We will feel powerless because we cannot keep a person with us, for they are on the road to somewhere else.

Our paths diverge. Loss is therefore inevitable. As Rachel Mann puts it, 'Perhaps loss is the price we all pay for being human, for being beautifully fragile. Indeed loss is one of the key marks of being human. In order for us to be human, things must change, things will and must get lost; we have to lose them in order to have new life and new possibilities.'[3]

Charlotte

'Religion has traditionally provided the ceremonies for birth and death, for naming and for loss. Increasingly religious institutions have been providing naming ceremonies for trans people. For some within the Christian tradition this has been linked to baptism whilst for others it has been more explicitly linked to naming.

In my experience this was where the dissonance between my partner's experience and my own was greatest. For him his naming service was a time of celebration and being able to authentically be recognised by the church, before God, as his true self. It was the ceremony at which the church itself committed to recognise his true identity and his ontological being. Yet, for me it was the ceremony marking the loss I felt. Yes, my partner is the same person but that person no longer had the same name, appearance or the same pronouns. I was simultaneously with the same person and with somebody completely different from the one I had first met and fallen in love with.

The complexity of these services and the way in which they have different meanings for different participants means that I believe they are important areas for future study by both the religious groups who offer these services and by the academy as it seeks to further understand the complexities of the whole trans experience, including for cis partners.'

*

Rachel Mann reflects on the impact upon her family and friends of her own transition from being Nick, 'They loved Nick, of course. And I destroyed him. My clothes, my voice, even my body, as it began to change, all were no longer Nick…I killed that boy. I killed that man. I became Rachel.'[4] Yet this losing of a life in order to save it was, for her, integrally connected with her life in God. As she describes it, 'Some things are irresistible. At Whitsun 1996 I was staying at my parents' when I simply could not resist any longer. The urge to pray was overwhelming and I let go. I remember saying, "God, if you are there, then I am yours." And as I dared to lose control, I sensed God was there. I felt like I was letting go of my carefully shaped control. Of my carefully crafted self. And I felt absurdly loved – utterly, unconditionally loved. For exactly who I was.'[5]

Going through a deep personal transformation, probably the deepest that can be imagined for a human being short of the transformation from life into death, put her in touch with the transformational love of God: 'I cannot quite explain how God's solidarity is transformative. Perhaps that's the point: the love which stands beside us, which bleeds with us, and will not walk away is beyond explanation. "Explanation" is the business of theories and analysis. Transformation is about experience.'(6)

We are human beings, flesh and blood, infinitely beloved of God, trying to learn how to love one another as God would have us love one another – with our hearts, souls, minds and bodies. Our different cultural locations, and our varying positions within power structures give us a diversity of experiences, and we need one another's perspectives to learn to be better at it. We need to discover how better to open our hearts to one another; to create spaces beyond convention where God can speak and live and do God's creative work.

Conclusion

> 'But we have this treasure in clay jars, so that it may
> be made clear that this extraordinary power belongs
> to God and does not come from us. We are afflicted in
> every way, but not crushed; perplexed, but not driven to
> despair; persecuted, but not forsaken; struck down, but
> not destroyed; always carrying in the body the death of
> Jesus, so that the life of Jesus may also be made visible in
> our bodies. For while we live, we are always being given
> up to death for Jesus' sake, so that the life of Jesus may
> be made visible in our mortal flesh. So death is at work
> in us, but life in you.'
> *(2 Corinthians 4: 7-12)*

This passage presents a key concluding theological insight that needs to speak into our conversations about sexuality and gender. We are fragile. We are jars made of the dust of the earth. The death of Jesus is carried in the body politic of marginalised people. But there is life, creativity and extraordinary power within each and every one of us.

As I have explored elsewhere[1] we live in an individualistic culture that assumes autonomy as our natural condition, to be valued above all else. This is our contextual reality. It tells us that from time to time in life – episodically – we will need to lean on others. If we are physically incapacitated or mentally unwell, for instance, or we lose a job and seek out the support of others to makes ends meet. These things are constructed as necessarily temporary. We will 'get back on our feet'. We will 'recover'. We will get better. The dependency of childhood is mere preparation for the autonomy of adulthood, and our education focuses on how we will negotiate that forthcoming reality. The frailty that comes with old age is something we deal with badly, for we see no cultural purpose in it.

The gospel requires that we reverse this understanding; that we see vulnerability as our contextual reality. We are other-dependent for our physical and emotional needs, for our sense of ourselves – our identity, our self-perception. Episodically we may experience a sense of self-sufficiency, but this is a culturally generated, economically-driven illusion. In reality we are hurt and broken by others, and held up by them. Others make us anxious and afraid, but also enable us to flourish. Speaking into this reality is the voice of God, exhorting us to 'fear not'. We are treasured. We are prized. We are cherished. We are loved. Loneliness and isolation are all around us in our contextual idolisation of autonomy and independence. We need a new language of kindness and acceptance – a still small voice that can silence the cultural message that we are not good enough, haven't achieved enough, haven't enough to show for our lives, that we are not enough. Contextual strength and episodic vulnerability breeds secrecy, stigma and shame. Contextual vulnerability and episodic strength breeds compassion and a relinquishing of the will to control.

Carl Rogers, psychologist and founder of the person-centred therapy movement, originally intended to be a Christian minister. The story of why he changed his mind is interesting. He was studying at Union Theological Seminary in New York in the 1920s, a progressive place back then, as it is today. However, '...increasingly he came to realise that, deeply as he was committed to the constructive improvement of life for society and for individuals, he could not stay in a field where he would be required to believe in a specific religious doctrine. The thought of having to profess a set of beliefs in order to remain in one's profession struck Rogers as something "horrible".'[2] He felt that Christianity in its institutional form could not embrace fully the authority of human experience, for belief systems would always come first. He therefore crossed the road – literally and metaphorically – to the Teachers' College of Columbia University, taking a course in clinical psychology.

The stories within this book show, again and again, that Rogers was right. In its approach to gender and sexuality institutional Christianity has prioritised control above compassion in order to protect certain inherited systems of belief. These systems are highly contested, and increasingly so, with no constructive or creative process in place for the experiences of marginalised people to be heard. The Church of England, for instance, has gone through a process known as 'Shared Conversations', but many LGBT people who have participated in this reflect that they were the ones under scrutiny, whilst heterosexual normativity was at no stage seriously problematised.

There are riches in Carl Rogers' approach that can enhance any conversation: one-to-one or collective – about who we are and how we live. His person-centred approach has been embraced in many spheres of life – not least in education, conflict resolution and organisational development. Rogers was nominated for the Nobel Peace Prize because of his commitment to the promotion of peace in many situations around the world. I think his approach gives us a framework for moving forward in our faith communities with sexuality and gender. Rogers famously names three conditions to promote human growth and flourishing. These are empathy (hearing and being heard), unconditional positive regard (prizing the other), and congruence (being real).

In explaining what he means by empathy, he reflects on why really hearing someone enriches one's life, 'When I say that I enjoy hearing someone, I mean, of course, hearing deeply. I mean that I hear the words, the thoughts, the feeling tones, the personal meaning, even the meaning that is below the conscious intent of the speaker…I hear a deep human cry that lies buried and unknown far below the surface of the person. So I have learned to ask myself, can I hear the sounds and sense the shape of this other person's inner world? Can I resonate to what he is saying so deeply that I sense the meanings he is afraid of yet would like to communicate, as well as those he knows?'[3] And then he describes how this feels from the other perspective,

> 'I like to *be heard*. A number of times in my life I have felt myself bursting with insoluble problems, or going round and round in tormented circles or, during one period, overcome by feelings of worthlessness and despair. I think I have been more fortunate than most in finding at these times individuals who have been able to hear me and thus to rescue me from the chaos of my feelings, individuals who have been able to hear my meanings a little more deeply than I have known them. These persons have heard me without judging me, diagnosing me, appraising me, evaluating me. They have just listened and clarified and responded to me at all the levels at which I was communicating… At these times it has relaxed the tension in me. It has permitted me to bring out the frightening feelings, the guilts, the despair, the confusions that have been part of my experience.'[4]

The process of writing this book has, for me, given a glimpse of what this means. Reading over and over and over, processing and editing the experiences of the women who shared their stories with me, has changed the ecology of my heart. They have entered my own psyche at a very deep level. A wise spiritual leader gave me a language for this when he said, 'you are doing really deep and difficult work – creating space for people to articulate experiences that are typically silenced in our church context. Holding that space is such an amazing spiritual practice. Thanks for creating space in your heart and soul for such a community to form. You are not alone in your heart. There, you hold a holy community of people who don't realise they belong together.'

Conclusion

As Christian communities we have not found ways to 'hear one another into speech' about who we are, because we have been too focused on what Rogers identifies as judgement, diagnosis, appraisal and evaluation. We have set up a relational ideal (which has a historicity all of its own, but most recently it has been heterosexual monogamous marriage), against which all other so-called 'lifestyles' are measured. Being tested and found wanting is something we do to ourselves as well as experiencing it from without, because the forms of control upon us are subtle and internalised. We end up with the ironic spectre of a faith that preaches a God of unconditional love – even unto death – whilst seeing only clay jars and totally missing the treasure.

Rogers has a word for that treasure, and how we value it. He calls it 'prizing another'. He says, 'I feel enriched when I can truly prize or care for or love another person and when I can let that feeling flow out to that person...I have too slowly learned that tender, positive feelings are not dangerous either to give or to receive.'[5] And the effects he describes from the receiver's perspective are equally dramatic, 'When I am prized, I blossom and expand, I am an interesting individual. In a hostile or unappreciative group, I am just not much of anything... Thus, prizing or loving and being prized or loved is experienced as growth enhancing. A person who is loved appreciatively, not possessively, blooms and develops his own unique self. The person who loves nonpossessively is himself enriched. This, at least, has been my experience.'[6]

What if 'mutual prizing' were to become our overarching criterion for recognising a good relationship when we see one? Rather than seeing only the likely life-span of the relationship, or the gender of the people involved. Surely Megan and Nel would represent something exemplary in such a schema for, as Megan expressed it to Nel in her wedding vows, 'With you I feel alive, at rest and free. With you I feel safe, cared for and protected, loved, listened to, and trusted, able to grow, to try, to make mistakes, to let go, to be myself. With you I feel precious and beautiful.'

Conclusion

We need to work towards faith communities replete with people who feel unconditionally loved by God in all aspects of our being, such that we overflow with unconditional love for others. We will love our bodies, accept them just as they are, care for and cherish them because they are fearfully and wonderfully made, and we will enjoy our embodiment. We will recognise our diversity and that we are interdependent and all have gifts and needs. Those who cannot 'enjoy' their embodiment because of chronic pain or disability will at least feel that they have a vital place in our community, and that we would be impoverished and incomplete without them. We will be a people who begin from an assumption that every person's sexuality is God's gift to them, in its uniqueness and in its mysterious and wonderful complexity. When we speak of it we will treat it as holy and sacred ground – to be approached with awe and wonder; as something intriguing, something to learn ever more of. And in seeking to learn, we will be able to speak freely and honestly because we are looking at God's creation together, and there can be no condemnation. We will notice and share our attractions and our desires; reflect on our commitments and the challenges to them that new forms of intimacy may bring. We will be able to support one another and reflect together on how to live out our feelings appropriately and express ourselves authentically. All of this becomes possible only when we begin by prizing, not judging.

What if 'mutual prizing' were also to become the foundation of our faith discussions about sexuality and gender? What if we could set up contexts in which we can appreciate one another, enable one another to blossom, expand and grow; where we do this together, intentionally, rather than despite one another. Rogers' third condition is important here – the ability to be real. He says this, 'I find it very satisfying when I can be real, when I can be close to whatever it is that is going on within me. I like it when I can listen to myself. To really know what I am experiencing in the moment is by no means an easy thing, but I feel somewhat encouraged because I think that over the years I have been improving at it. I am convinced, however, that it is a lifelong task and that none of us ever is totally able to be comfortably close to all that is going on within our own experience.'[7]

Rogers holds out the possibility of learning to be honest and real, and to get better at it. The twists and turns of ecclesiastical politics have strewn many obstacles to authenticity in our path. We all suffer because of them. It has fallen to those who are most vulnerable; those who are marginalised by the rules as they currently are, to speak openly and honestly of their experience in inhospitable contexts. This has often been painful, and there is little evidence that the vulnerable have felt heard. But when experience is shared in safe-enough spaces, as in the context of this book, the learnings can be astounding. Power structures make such sharing difficult, as much for those deeply embedded in them as for those in exile from them. What we share is the temptation to fear. Those with privilege often inhabit it with a sense of ambivalence; afraid of not being up to the task entrusted to them, or of losing their positions. Those locked out of it feel a sense of injustice, and a fear that power will be used against them.

But our faith is counter-cultural. Again and again we are exhorted by God to 'fear not'. Whilst I cannot speak for all the women in this book, I suspect strongly that they would join me in issuing an invitation to all of us, whatever our combination of power and powerlessness, to step forward and risk the vulnerability of hearing others and of being heard; of sharing our questions, struggles and doubts; to risk finding freedom in being known, accepted and loved. For it is only as a community of the vulnerable, standing together, that we can bring any sense of God's love and fullness of life to our world. I venture to say, with the community that built this book: don't just hear us. Join us.

Notes

Introduction

1. Lightsey, P. (2015) *Our Lives Matter: A Womanist Queer Theology*, Eugene, OR: Pickwick Publications, p. 49 to 50.
2. *Issues in Human Sexuality: A Statement by the House of Bishops* (1991), London: Church House Publishing.

Chapter One: Found Out

1. Webster, A. (1995) *Found Wanting: Women, Christianity and Sexuality*, London: Cassell.
2. Miles, S. (2012) *Take This Bread*, London: Canterbury Press.
3. Nelson, J. (2005) *Seeing Through Tears: Crying and Attachment*, New York and Hove: Routledge, p. 6.
4. Nelson, J. (2005) *Seeing Through Tears: Crying and Attachment*, New York and Hove: Routledge, p. 195–6.
5. Nelson, J. (2005) *Seeing Through Tears: Crying and Attachment*, New York and Hove: Routledge, p. 136.

Chapter Two: Retrospective

1. Dummett, A. (1973) *A Portrait of English Racism*, London: Penguin.
2. Bailey, S. (1996) *The Well Within: Parables for Living and Dying*, London: Darton, Longman and Todd.
3. Woodward, J. (ed.) (1990) *Embracing the Chaos: Theological Responses to AIDS*, London: SPCK.
4. Webster, A. (ed.) (1988) *Just Love: A Resource Book Exploring the Theology of Sexuality*, Birmingham: Student Christian Movement.

5. Nelson, J. (1988) *The Intimate Connection: Male Sexuality, Masculine Spirituality*, Louisville: Westminster John Knox Press.
6. Pryce, M. (1993) *Men, Masculinity and Pastoral Care*, imprint unknown.
7. Adams, C. (1990 and 2015) *The Sexual Politics of Meat: A Feminist-Vegetarian Critical Theory*, New York: Bloomsbury.
8. Adams, C. (1997) *Ecofeminism and the Sacred*, London and New York: Continuum International Publishing.
9. Morley, J. (2005) *All Desires Known*, London: SPCK (first published in 1988 by Women in Theology).
10. St Hilda Community (1991) *Women Included, A Book of Prayers and Services*. Reissued by SPCK in 1996, edited by Monica Furlong.
11. *Theology and Sexuality*, Abingdon: Taylor and Francis, from 1994.
12. Greenfield, S. (2008) *ID: The Quest for Meaning in the Twenty First Century*, London: Sceptre.
13. Lightsey, P. (2015) *Our Lives Matter: A Womanist Queer Theology*, Eugene, OR: Pickwick Publications, pp. 49–50.
14. Unstrangemind: remapping my world blog can be found at: https://unstrangemind.wordpress.com/2013/01/27/no-you-dont/)

Chapter Three: Resistance

1. O'Brien, M. (2016) 'Intersex, Medicine, Diversity, Identity and Spirituality' in Beardsley, C. and O'Brien, M. (eds) *This is my Body: Hearing the Theology of Transgender Christians*, London: Darton, Longman and Todd, pp. 45–55.

Chapter Four: Reclaiming Spirit

1. Mann, R. (2012) *Dazzling Darkness*, Glasgow: Wild Goose Publications, p. 90 and p. 92.
2. O'Brien, M. (2016) 'Intersex, Medicine, Diversity, Identity and Spirituality' in Beardsley, C. and O'Brien, M. (eds) *This is my Body: Hearing the Theology of Transgender Christians*, London: Darton, Longman and Todd, pp. 45–55, p. 54.

Notes

Chapter Five: Recreating Faith

1. McLaren, B. (2016) *The Great Spiritual Migration: How the World's largest Religion is Seeking a Better Way to be Christian*, London: Hodder and Stoughton, p. 2-3.
2. Webster, A. (2009) *You Are Mine: Reflections on Who We Are*, London: SPCK, especially the chapter on Faith, pp 80-115.
3. McLaren, B. (2016) *The Great Spiritual Migration: How the World's Largest Religion is Seeking a Better Way to be Christian*, London: Hodder and Stoughton, p. 33.
4. Kosofsky Sedgwick, E. (1994) *Tendencies*, London: Routledge.
5. Kosofsky Sedgwick, E. (1994) *Tendencies*, London: Routledge, p. 8.
6. Rudy, K. 'Subjectivity and Belief' in Loughlin, G. (ed.) (2007) *Queer Theology: Rethinking the Western Body*, Oxford: Blackwell, pp 37-49.
7. Rudy, K. 'Subjectivity and Belief' in Loughlin, G. (ed.) (2007) *Queer Theology: Rethinking the Western Body*, Oxford: Blackwell, pp 37-49, p. 38.
8. Rudy, K. 'Subjectivity and Belief' in Loughlin, G. (ed.) (2007) Queer Theology: Rethinking the Western Body, Oxford: Blackwell, pp 37-49, p. 38, p. 43.
9. Butler, J. 'Imitation and Gender Insubordination', in Fuss, D. (ed.) (1991) *Inside Out: Lesbian Theories/Gay Theories*, London: Routledge, pp. 13-31, p.18.
10. Butler, J. 'Imitation and Gender Insubordination', in Fuss, D. (ed.) (1991) *Inside Out: Lesbian Theories/Gay Theories*, London: Routledge, pp. 13-31, p. 23-4.
11. Rudy, K. 'Subjectivity and Belief' in Loughlin, G. (ed.) (2007) *Queer Theology: Rethinking the Western Body*, Oxford: Blackwell, pp 37-49, p. 38, p. 45.
12. Haraway, D. (1991) 'Situated Knowledges: The Science Question in Feminism and the Privilege of Partial Perspective' in *Simians, Cyborgs and Women: The Reinvention of Nature*, London: Free Association Books, pp. 183-201, p. 186.
13. Webster, A. (2009) *You Are Mine: Reflections on Who We Are*, London: SPCK, p. 89.

14. Haraway, D. (1991) 'Situated Knowledges: The Science Question in Feminism and the Privilege of Partial Perspective' in *Simians, Cyborgs and Women: The Reinvention of Nature*, London: Free Association Books, pp. 183–201, p.188.
15. Haraway, D. (1991) 'Situated Knowledges: The Science Question in Feminism and the Privilege of Partial Perspective' in *Simians, Cyborgs and Women: The Reinvention of Nature*, London: Free Association Books, pp. 183–201, p.191.
16. Lightsey, P. (2015) *Our Lives Matter: A Womanist Queer Theology*, Eugene, OR: Pickwick Publications, p. 37–8.
17. Lightsey, P. (2015) *Our Lives Matter: A Womanist Queer Theology*, Eugene, OR: Pickwick Publications, p. 39.
18. Mann, R. (2012) *Dazzling Darkness*, Glasgow: Wild Goose Publications, p. 27.
19. Cheng, P. (2011) *Radical Love: An Introduction to Queer Theology*, New York: Seabury Books, p. 9
20. Loughlin, G. (2007) 'Introduction: The End of Sex' in Loughlin, G. *Queer Theology: Rethinking the Western Body*, Oxford: Blackwell, Oxford, p. 7 and p. 9
21. Mann, R. (2012) *Dazzling Darkness*, Glasgow: Wild Goose Publications, p. 25–8.
22. Mann, R. (2012) *Dazzling Darkness*, Glasgow: Wild Goose Publications, p. 29
23. Alison, J. (2007) 'The Gay Thing: Following the Still Small Voice' in Loughlin, G. (ed.) *Queer Theology: Rethinking the Western Body*, Oxford: Blackwell, pp. 50–62, p. 51
24. Mann, R. (2012) *Dazzling Darkness*, Glasgow: Wild Goose Publications, p. 29
25. Mann, R. (2012) *Dazzling Darkness*, Glasgow: Wild Goose Publications, p. 116–17.

Chapter Six: Remaking Love

1. Lorde, A. (1982), *Zami: A New Spelling of My Name*, Berkeley: The Crossing Press.

2. Ind, J. (2010) *Memories of Bliss: God, Sex and Us,* London: SCM Press.
3. Mann, R. (2012) *Dazzling Darkness,* Glasgow: Wild Goose Publications, p. 41.
4. Mann, R. (2012) *Dazzling Darkness,* Glasgow: Wild Goose Publications, p. 40.
5. Mann, R. (2012) *Dazzling Darkness,* Glasgow: Wild Goose Publications, p. 45.
6. Mann, R. (2012) *Dazzling Darkness,* Glasgow: Wild Goose Publications, p. 67.

Conclusion

1. Webster, A. (2002) *Wellbeing,* London: SCM Press.
2. Thorne, B. and Sanders, P. (2013) *Carl Rogers,* London: Sage, p. 6.
3. Rogers, C. (1995), *A Way of Being,* Boston and New York: Houghton Mifflin Company, p. 8
4. Rogers, C. (1995), *A Way of Being,* Boston and New York: Houghton Mifflin Company, p. 12.
5. Rogers, C. (1995), *A Way of Being,* Boston and New York: Houghton Mifflin Company, p. 20.
6. Rogers, C. (1995), *A Way of Being,* Boston and New York: Houghton Mifflin Company, p. 23.
7. Rogers, C. (1995), *A Way of Being,* Boston and New York: Houghton Mifflin Company, p. 14.